BUREAU OF SAFETY AND ENVIRONMENTAL ENFORCEMENT

FY 2014 GREENBOOK

Table of Contents

Director's Preface

FY 2014 PERFORMANCE JUSTIFICATIONS
Bureau of Safety and Environmental Enforcement
Director's Preface

As the Administration works to expand domestic energy production through President Obama's "All of the Above" strategy, the Bureau of Safety and Environmental Enforcement (BSEE) is taking the necessary steps to provide effective oversight of oil and gas development on the U.S. Outer Continental Shelf (OCS), promoting compliance with Federal regulations, and leading the offshore oil and gas industry toward a culture of safety and environmental protection.

Since BSEE's establishment on October 1, 2011, we have been working to institutionalize the regulatory reforms put into place during the aftermath of the 2010 *Deepwater Horizon* explosion and oil spill, and fully establish the new Bureau. The President's Fiscal Year (FY) 2014 request will provide the funds to substantially complete the Bureau build-out and ensure the tremendous enhancements to safety and environmental protection that have been achieved do not become obsolete. Through this request, BSEE will continue to put in place the tools necessary to effectively guide industry to safely develop oil and gas resources, utilizing both new technologies and sound management practices as operations move into deeper water and encounter greater temperatures and pressures.

Our guiding principle is "Safety at All Levels, at All Times" as we work to lead the industry toward offshore excellence. Our efforts are supported by two strategic goals:

- Regulate, enforce, and respond to OCS development using the full range of authorities, policies, and tools to compel safety, emergency preparedness, and environmental responsibility, and appropriate development and conservation of the offshore oil and natural gas resources, and;

- Build and sustain the organizational, technical, and intellectual capacity within and across BSEE's key functions – capacity that keeps pace with OCS industry technological improvements, innovates in regulation and enforcement, and reduces risk through systemic assessment and regulatory and enforcement actions.

These strategic goals guide our decision-making and investment strategies. The FY 2014 request furthers these goals by providing the capacity in existing offices in multiple disciplines to staff regulatory, safety management, environmental compliance, structural and technical support, and oil spill response programs. We will build independent and dependable inspection capabilities in Alaska to support the anticipated growth in exploration, development, and production activities in that Region. We will continue to enhance our information systems to support the development of a modern electronic system for conducting offshore inspections and real-time monitoring. And, we will address key knowledge and technology gaps in oil spill response through a robust technology research agenda.

The President's commitment to the responsible development of our Nation's domestic energy resources is realized through a clear regulatory framework: an efficient, yet rigorous permitting process; effective monitoring and oversight; and the consistent application of a comprehensive enforcement strategy. Without these critical elements, supported by the necessary staffing, training, and resources, the industry will lack the certainty and predictability needed to make decisions, while the risks to worker safety and to the environment will unacceptably increase.

This page intentionally left blank.

General Statement

FY 2014 PERFORMANCE BUDGET
Bureau of Safety and Environmental Enforcement
General Statement

Table 1 : Summary of BSEE Budget Request

Account/Activity	FY 2013 Full Year CR	FY 2012 Enacted	FY 2014 Request	Changes from FY 2012
Offshore Safety and Environmental Enforcement (OSEE)				
Environmental Enforcement	4,117	4,108	8,314	+4,206
Operations, Safety and Regulation	132,306	132,079	147,282	+15,203
Administrative Operations	15,576	15,545	19,605	+4,060
General Support Services	12,631	12,607	13,911	+1,304
Executive Direction	18,202	18,117	18,121	+4
Total, OSEE	**182,832**	**182,456**	**207,233**	**+24,777**
Offsetting Rental Receipts	-52,587	-52,587	-50,568	+2,019
Cost Recovery	-6,494	-6,494	-8,402	-1,908
Inspection Fees	-62,000	-62,000	-65,000	-3,000
Total, Offsetting Collections	**-121,081**	**-121,081**	**-123,970**	**-2,889**
Net OSEE	**61,751**	**61,375**	**83,263**	**+21,888**
Oil Spill Research	**14,990**	**14,899**	**14,899**	**0**
Disaster Relief Appropriations Act, 2013 (P.L. 113-2)	**3,000**			
Current BSEE Funding	**79,741**	**76,274**	**98,162**	**+21,888**
Total BSEE Funding	**200,822**	**197,355**	**222,132**	**+24,777**
Full Time Equivalents (FTE)				
Total Direct FTE	585	519	638	+119
Total Reimbursable FTE (Reimbursable Agreements) [1]	125	96	125	+29
Total FTE [2/,3/]	**710**	**615**	**763**	**+148**

[1/] BSEE has changed the manner in which it is reporting FTE funded by offsetting collections to show them in the direct category as of FY 2013.

[2/] 2012 FTE amounts reflect actual usage, not 2012 enacted formulation estimates.

[3/] The total FTE increase estimated for FY 2014 is 69 FTE. The technical adjustment of 79 FTE represents the difference between 2012 actual and enacted FTE as a result of challenges filling vacant technical positions.

The Outer Continental Shelf (OCS) is a major source of energy for the United States. In calendar year 2011, OCS leases offshore California, Alaska, and in the Gulf of Mexico provided about 501 million barrels of oil and 1,892 billion cubic feet of natural gas, accounting for almost 24 percent of the Nation's oil production and over 6 percent of domestic natural gas production.

The Bureau of Safety and Environmental Enforcement (BSEE) is responsible for the oversight of exploration, development, and production operations for oil and natural gas on the OCS. BSEE's regulation and oversight of Federal offshore resources ensures that the OCS remains a solid contributor to the Nation's energy needs through safe and environmentally-responsible oil and gas development and the conservation of resources.

The functions of BSEE include oil and gas permitting, facility inspections, regulations and standards development, safety research, environmental compliance and enforcement, oil spill preparedness compliance and enforcement, production and development oversight, conservation of resources, and operation of a national training program.

FY 2014 PERFORMANCE BUDGET REQUEST

 **BSEE works to promote safety, protect the environment, and conserve resources offshore through vigorous regulatory oversight and enforcement.**

On May 19, 2010, Secretary of the Interior Ken Salazar signed Secretarial Order 3329, dividing the Minerals Management Service (MMS) into three independent entities to better carry out its three core missions: ensuring the balanced and responsible development of energy resources on the OCS; ensuring safe and environmentally responsible exploration and production and enforcing applicable rules and regulations; and ensuring a fair return to the taxpayer from royalty and revenue collection and disbursement activities.

In the place of the former MMS, three strong, independent agencies with clearly defined roles and missions were created. The Office of Natural Resources Revenue began operations on October 1, 2010, with the mission of collecting and disbursing revenues from domestic energy production while ensuring a fair return to the taxpayer from that production. An interim agency, the Bureau of Ocean Energy Management, Regulation and Enforcement (BOEMRE), was responsible for the remaining MMS functions during FY 2011. The Bureau of Ocean Energy Management (BOEM) and the Bureau of Safety and Environmental Enforcement (BSEE) formally began independent operations on October 1, 2011, with distinct concepts, missions, and functions relevant to each Bureau. BOEM's mission is responsible for managing overall development of energy resources on the Outer Continental Shelf (OCS) in an environmentally and economically responsible way. BSEE's mission is to oversee safety and environmental enforcement for OCS operations to ensure compliance with applicable rules and regulations.

Progress through Reforms

FY 2014 represents the third year of operations for BSEE. This request is guided by the newly developed BSEE FY 2012-2015 Strategic Plan which includes two strategic goals to guide the Bureau in accomplishing its mission. This strategic plan is a result of a planning process that included a review of legacy documents, industry reports, and input from senior leadership. The two goals are:

- To regulate, enforce, and respond to Outer Continental Shelf (OCS) development using the full range of authorities, policies, and tools to compel safety, emergency preparedness and environmental responsibility and appropriate development and conservation of the offshore oil and natural gas resources.

- To build and sustain the organizational, technical, and intellectual capacity within and across BSEE's key functions – capacity that keeps pace with the OCS industry's technological improvements, innovates in regulation and enforcement, and reduces risk through systemic assessment and regulatory and enforcement actions.

The BSEE Strategic Plan encapsulates the intent of BSEE to keep pace with the rapidly advancing technologies employed by the industry; build and sustain internal organizational, technical, and intellectual capacity; and commit to instilling safe practices at all levels of offshore operations, at all times.

Below are some of BSEE's key goals of investments:

- Continue to enhance offshore safety and environmental performance by promoting a safety culture within the offshore oil and gas industry.

- Promote and support innovation through the use of Best Available and Safest Technology (BAST) within the drilling, production and spill response stakeholder communities.

- Promote compliance through strategic enforcement by fully defining, enhancing, and utilizing the Bureau's enforcement authorities with a specific focus on risk.

- Invest in BSEE employees through recruiting and training.

- Promote the use of information, including real time monitoring, to enhance safety and environmental protection.

The Bureau successfully implemented significant reforms in FY 2012 that addressed several of the major recommendations resulting from the investigations and reports that followed the tragic explosion of the *Deepwater Horizon* and the subsequent oil spill. The Bureau issued the final drilling safety regulations put in place on an interim basis after the spill and also updated oil spill response planning guidance; both of these reforms will contribute to the overall safety of the offshore oil and gas industry. In cooperation with industry, BSEE also conducted the first ever full-scale deployment drill for a deepwater containment system.

The achievements represent important steps to promote offshore safety, protect the environment, and conserve resources. As planned, the Bureau continues to implement reforms and to hire the needed personnel. These continued reforms and addition of highly qualified staff are essential to establishing a culture of safety and achieving the efficiency and effectiveness envisioned.

Due to the challenges presented by the reorganization and reform efforts, the Bureau ended FY 2012 with fewer onboard personnel than anticipated and has developed an execution plan for FY 2013 and FY 2014 that will enable the Bureau to aggressively pursue personnel and system improvements. BSEE will apply existing resources to projects and activities that will address its strategic goals while allowing the Bureau to continue recruiting critical personnel.

BSEE will focus funding on projects that will enhance the systems and protocols necessary to implement real-time monitoring capabilities, risk-based inspections, and advanced inspection technologies. BSEE will also pursue incorporation of BAST including technology testing by independent laboratories that will reduce reliance on industry to verify the efficacy of emerging technology. Additional investments will focus on oil spill response and preparedness and major improvements to the Bureau's data management systems.

Compliance and Inspections

A key component of the reorganization and reform efforts begun in FY 2011 is the identification of how BSEE can improve its regulatory, inspection and compliance programs. Based on recommendations from investigatory and oversight reports, internal and external review of operations, and reorganization studies, BSEE has already implemented a number of improvements to its inspection regime and will continually look for improvements to enhance its programs.

Safety is a priority for both BSEE staff and for the operations that occur under BSEE's jurisdiction. Onsite facility inspections and enforcement actions are important components of BSEE's safety program. The Bureau has established ambitious performance targets for the conduct of thousands of inspections of OCS facilities and operations, including coverage of tens of thousands of safety and pollution prevention components each year to prevent offshore accidents and spills, and to ensure a safe working environment. In recent years, BSEE has adopted a goal of conducting monthly inspections of OCS drilling facilities, and therefore providing additional oversight to these specialized facilities.

These increases in inspection/oversight, most notably on drilling operations, combined with the increase in OCS oil and gas activities in the Gulf of Mexico, Pacific, and Alaska Regions, have required that BSEE increase its inspector workforce and grow their skill base.

BSEE is also actively working to develop a risk-based inspection methodology for use at various levels within the regulatory program. The Bureau plans to use the information gleaned from an ongoing risk correlation analysis to learn more about the relative risks posed by discrete offshore oil and gas activities. BSEE will then use the updated risk model to identify and focus Bureau inspections on the "riskiest" activities.

Safety and Environmental Management: The Safety and Environmental Management System (SEMS) is a nontraditional, performance-focused tool for integrating and managing operations on the OCS. Following the *Deepwater Horizon* event, BSEE instituted regulations requiring OCS operators to have SEMS systems in place. BSEE continues to make strides in safety and environmental management and has recently finalized "Revision to Safety and Environmental Management Systems", or SEMS II. SEMS II addresses safety concerns that were not addressed in the original SEMS rule.

Real-Time Monitoring: BSEE is also actively reviewing the use of Real Time Monitoring (RTM) as a regulatory tool. The intent of RTM is to develop, test, and implement reforms that significantly improve the Inspection and Enforcement Program in BSEE by using innovative technologies and using risk-based inspection criteria to supplement BSEE's current inspection program. The use of RTM technology and facilities to monitor OCS oil and gas drilling, well-completion, well workover, well servicing and other rig related operations is one avenue to help meet the BSEE mission. BSEE is also considering other RTM opportunities not associated with onshore monitoring facilities.

BSEE is currently working to determine which available RTM opportunities would provide the best return on investment and which activities require on-site inspectors. Initially, the focus will be on high risk activities involving deepwater drilling and casing/cementing. The use of RTM will allow BSEE to quickly shift technical resources to evaluate these operations wherever they occur.

Emerging Technologies (formerly Technology Assessment and Research): BSEE continues to promote identification of and use of BAST associated with energy and mineral operations, ranging from the drilling of oil and gas exploration wells in search of new reserves to the removal of platforms and related infrastructure once production operations have ceased. Under the Emerging Technologies Program, BSEE promotes the investigation of new technologies to promote safe operations, prevention of oil pollution, and the improvement of oil spill response and clean-up.

Beginning in FY2012, BSEE focused its efforts to identify high-risk components and systems, such as blowout preventers (BOPs), to ensure that industry was applying BAST in those areas where overall risks could be reduced. To take advantage of and leverage expertise from other Federal resources, BSEE has entered into an Interagency Agreement (IAA) with the Department of Energy National Laboratory system to collaborate on risk-based decision making and applying BAST to offshore components, systems and procedures.

FY 2014 BUDGET HIGHLIGHTS

BSEE receives funding through the Offshore Safety and Environmental Enforcement (OSEE) and Oil Spill Research (OSR) appropriations. The OSEE appropriation is partially offset by a portion of OCS rental collections, cost recovery fees, and inspection fees. The OSR appropriation is funded through the Oil Spill Liability Trust Fund.

In FY 2014, the BSEE budget requests $222.1 million which includes $50.6 million from offsetting rental collections, $8.4 million from cost recovery fees, and $65 million from inspection fees.

The budget for BSEE in the OSEE account funds the following activities:

- The ***Environmental Enforcement*** Activity funds: environmental compliance activities related to issuing permits associated with plans; inspections of environmental measures and enforcement of incidences of noncompliance; and monitoring industry compliance with mitigation and other environmental requirements through office and field inspections.

- The ***Operations, Safety and Regulation*** Activity funds: OCS permit application reviews; inspections of OCS facilities including critical high-risk activities; offshore operator oil spill planning and preparedness compliance; accident investigations; civil penalties and operator disqualification; operator training and audit programs; annual operator performance reviews; verification of oil and gas production levels to help ensure the public receives a fair return; and the Emerging Technologies Program (formerly the Technology Assessment and Research Program).

- The ***Administrative Operations*** Activity funds: general administration and ethics; equal employment opportunity services; emergency management; finance; human resources; procurement; and information management. BSEE provides administrative services, such as human resources, procurement, and finance to BOEM and other entities within the Department.

- The ***General Support Services*** Activity funds: shared activities and related support services for the Bureau. These include expenses such as: rental and security of office space; workers' compensation and unemployment compensation; voice and data communications; centrally provided services funded by the Department's Working Capital Fund; annual building maintenance contracts; mail services; and printing costs. BSEE will continue to provide some of these services to BOEM through a reimbursable service agreement.

- The ***Executive Direction*** Activity funds: Bureau-wide leadership, direction, management, coordination, communications strategies, and outreach. It includes functions such as budget, congressional and public affairs, and policy and analysis. The Office of the Director and the Regional Director's Offices are also funded within this activity.

The budget for BSEE in the OSR account funds oil spill research, oil spill response research, the Ohmsett facility, as well as oil spill response and planning.

Table 2: FY 2014 Analysis of Budgetary Changes

Bureau of Safety and Environmental Enforcement FY 2014 Budget Initiatives ($000)			
Organization/Category	Initiative	($000)	FTE [1,2]
BSEE FY 2012 ENACTED -- DIRECT APPROPRIATION		**76,274**	**615**
Offshore Safety and Environmental Enforcement (OSEE)			
Environmental Enforcement	Fixed Costs	+50	
	Management Efficiencies	-21	
	Strengthen Environmental Enforcement Program	+4,177	+14
	FTE Technical Adjustment		+9
Operations, Safety, and Regulation	Fixed Costs	+966	
	Management Efficiencies	-838	
	Research and Development for Offshore Drilling	+2,000	
	Operational Safety	+4,495	+33
	National Offshore Training Program	+3,685	+7
	Wellbore Integrity	+1,395	+9
	Alaska Program Growth	+2,500	+6
	Efficiencies in the permitting process: ePermits	+1,000	
	FTE Technical Adjustment		+51
Administrative Operations	Fixed Costs	+471	
	Management Efficiencies	-456	
	Sustain Administrative Operations	+4,045	
	FTE Technical Adjustment		+4
General Support Services	Fixed Costs	+2,690	
	Management Efficiencies	-1,386	
Executive Direction	Fixed Costs	+118	
	Management Efficiencies	-114	
	FTE Technical Adjustment		+10
	Subtotal of OSEE	**+24,777**	**+143**
	Changes in Offsetting Collections	-2,889	
Oil Spill Research Appropriation			
	FTE Technical Adjustment		+5
FY 2014 Requested Increase		+21,888	+148
BSEE FY 2014 PROPOSAL -- DIRECT APPROPRIATION		**98,162**	**763**

[1] 2012 FTE amounts reflect actual usage, not 2012 enacted formulation estimates.

[2] The total FTE increase estimated for FY 2014 is 69 FTE. The technical adjustment of 79 FTE represents the difference between 2012 actual and enacted FTE as a result of challenges filling vacant technical positions.

The following funding increases and decreases are proposed:

Fixed Costs (+$4,295,000): Projected fixed costs such as rent, salary increases, central billing, and information technology transformation for the Department's working capital fund, and other items are fully funded by this request.

Management Efficiencies (-$2,815,000): Programs will absorb these costs through greater efficiencies, cost savings, and administrative adjustments.

Strengthen Environmental Enforcement Program (+4,177,000; +14 FTE): Funding provided in FY 2012 enabled the hiring of initial personnel necessary to develop and manage the program, and ensure that the NEPA process requirements necessary to responsibly issue permits to conduct various offshore activities were met in each of the OCS regions. BSEE is requesting additional base funding needed to continue implementation of the enforcement program.

Research and Development for Offshore Drilling Safety (+$2,000,000; 0 FTE): Requests funding to perform additional, and more in-depth, research relating to safety systems and operations. As the industry pushes into deeper water and is drilling more high-pressure/high-temperature wells, current safety practices and technologies require continuous improvement to better ensure the integrity of equipment and operations.

Operational Safety (+$4,495,000; +33 FTE): Funds will support ongoing reorganization efforts identified as critical to the success of BSEE in strengthening post-*Deepwater Horizon* regulatory and oversight capabilities. It represents a cross section of staffing for newly identified efforts and increased activities such as development of regulations, safety management, structural and technical support, and oil spill response.

National Offshore Training Program (+$3,685,000; +7 FTE): This will provide base funding for the National Offshore Training Program (NOTP). The NOTP supports the Bureau's goals by providing upfront and ongoing learning and development opportunities to Bureau engineering and inspection staff. The NOTP will provide a wide variety of credible and up-to-date training programs designed to enhance the abilities of BSEE staff to address technological advances. Courses are selected and developed with a focus on BSEE's mission and vision of advancing safety and environmental stewardship principles using the best science and technology available to evaluate, protect, and preserve the human, marine, and coastal environments.

Wellbore Integrity (+$1,395,000; +9 FTE): Requested funding will provide resources needed for BSEE to meet current requirements to evaluate whether operators have submitted adequate information demonstrating access and deployment capabilities for surface and subsea containment.

Alaska Program Growth (+2,500,000; +6 FTE): This budget request will build independent and dependable inspection capabilities for significantly expanded drilling activity anticipated on the Alaska OCS; build basic engineering support for platform and pipeline functions; build basic engineering and geoscience support for unitization, reservoir and conservation functions; and build administrative support for the increasing volume of administrative files and complex processes for growth in the Alaska Region.

Efficiencies in the permitting process: ePermits (+$1,000,000; 0 FTE): BSEE requests additional funding to continue to enhance the management of the permitting process by providing a means for industry to submit permits on-line via the web and to better track the permit review process. In addition to web-based receipt of these documents and data, ePermits will provide the capability to track the evaluation of permits throughout the review process.

Sustain Administrative Operations (+$4,045,000; 0 FTE): Funding is needed to sustain the necessary level of support services for both BSEE and BOEM. The funding will be used to retain the expertise and personnel that will serve both Bureaus as they recruit new inspectors, engineers, scientists, and other disciplines needed to support the Bureaus' mission.

FTE Technical Adjustment (+79 FTE): The total FTE increase estimated for FY 2014 is 69 FTE. The technical adjustment of 79 FTE represents the difference between 2012 actual and enacted FTE as a result of challenges filling vacant technical positions. No additional funding is requested/associated with this adjustment.

Changes in Offsetting Collections (-$2,889,000, 0 FTE):

- **Rental Receipts (-$2,019,000; 0 FTE):** This decrease in rental receipts revenue results from an anticipated decrease of $2.0 million from the FY 2012 enacted amount of $52.6 million. This is one type of offsetting collection credited to the BSEE OSEE account to help defray the cost of operations. Also, included as offsetting collections are cost recovery and inspection fees.

- **Cost Recovery Fees (+$1,908,000; 0 FTE):** This increase in cost recovery fee revenue results from an anticipated increase of $1.9 million from the FY 2012 enacted amount of $6.5 million. This is one type of offsetting collection credited to the BSEE OSEE account to help defray the cost of operations. Also included as offsetting collections are certain rental receipts and inspection fees.

- **Inspection Fees (+$3,000,000; 0 FTE):** This increase in offsetting inspection fee revenue results from an anticipated increase of $3.0 million from the FY 2012 enacted amount of $62.0 million. This is one type of offsetting collection credited to the BSEE OSEE account to help defray the cost of operations. Also included as offsetting collections are certain rental receipts and cost recovery fees.

PERFORMANCE SUMMARY

BSEE aims to promote safety, protect the environment, and conserve resources offshore through vigorous regulatory oversight and enforcement.

Performance Management

BSEE's mission directly supports the Department of the Interior's Strategic Goal and Strategy to *Secure America's Energy Resources* while *ensuring environmental compliance and the safety of energy development.*

In FY 2013, BSEE undertook the following key strategies to strengthen regulatory oversight and enforcement of offshore energy development activities.

- Continued to reform and implement an expanded inspection and operational oversight regime, including the hiring of additional inspectors and the observing of selected high-risk drilling activities and tests
- Continued the establishment and implementation of a new environmental enforcement program to ensure compliance with relevant laws and to minimize the risk of environmental accidents
- Moved toward proactive enforcement capabilities to catch oil spill under-reporting, non-reporting, and delinquent Oil Spill Response Plan holders for enforcement actions.
- Conducted audits of the newly required SEMS regulation to ensure compliance and to increase offshore operational safety

- Expanded technical capabilities and resources for reviewing and processing drilling, production, and decommissioning permits
- Conducted targeted research on deepwater safety and spill containment utilizing research results to inform rulemaking, investigations, and plan reviews
- Expanded technical capabilities for oil spill research, risk analysis, and response planning
- Worked to begin implementing a mix of performance-based and prescriptive safety and pollution prevention standards to better assess and manage risk and to promote continuous improvement offshore.
- Continued the development and implementation of an offshore training center program with a certification process for inspectors, engineers, and other compliance personnel.

Performance for Key Increases

BSEE's FY 2014 proposal continues to advance the Secretary's objectives for strengthening the Nation's energy security while ensuring operational safety and environmental compliance. The FY 2014 funding increases will be used to:

- Increase Federal oversight of environmental compliance by establishing and maintaining BSEE's field environmental compliance, inspections, SEMS audits, investigations and enforcement capabilities;
- Further strengthen regulatory oversight by hiring the personnel needed to maintain up-to-date drilling-safety requirements that stay current with industry's rapidly evolving deepwater technology;
- Improve the Nation's preparedness posture for offshore oil spills by continuing to implement an integrated oil spill program that encompasses all aspects of oil discharge research and spill prevention, planning, and preparedness;
- Further expand the new training organization that is aimed at ensuring BSEE staff has the knowledge and skills necessary to execute a more consistent and effective inspection and compliance program;
- Ensure more timely and accurate collection of inspection data by replacing the outdated paper-based inspection process with a modern electronic system, which will also give inspectors immediate access to tools such as online policy manuals, Federal Regulations, Notice to Lessees (NTLs), Safety Alerts, and approved permits; and
- Conduct additional wellbore integrity evaluations to determine if casing design is adequate and minimizes the likelihood that hydrocarbons could be released to the sea floor in the event a blowout results in containment equipment being triggered.

Related program performance metric information can be found within the Goal Performance Table.

This page intentionally left blank.

Bureau of Safety and Environmental Enforcement
Secretarial Initiatives, Agency Priority Goals, and
Administration Management Initiatives

The Bureau of Safety and Environmental Enforcement fully supports the Secretarial and Administration Initiatives to realize agency goals and implement the Administration's management initiatives. BSEE contributes to these efforts in several ways.

Secretarial Initiative: Information Technology Transformation
The FY 2014 President's Budget Request includes $185,500 for BSEE participation in the Department's IT Transformation efforts through the Department's Working Capital Fund. These funds will support IT Transformation project-level planning and coordination and the implementation of enterprise IT services.

Agency Priority Goal: Youth in the Great Outdoors
Goal: By September 30, 2013, the Department of the Interior will maintain the increased level of employment of individuals between the ages of 15 to 25 that was achieved in FY 2010 (35 percent increase in total youth employment over FY 2009) to support the Department's mission of natural and cultural resource management. For FY 2014, the Department is expecting to sustain a level of youth engagement similar to that achieved in FY 2010 (35 percent increase in total youth employment over FY 2009), based on estimated funding and participation from partners through the 21st Century Conservation Service Corps (CSC).

In its first year, BSEE has taken a number of steps to attract, retain, and train younger employees that provided management of oil and gas activities on the OCS. These include the following:

- Recruitment Teams - BSEE has recruitment teams throughout its regional offices that target engineers and scientists at the entry level and mid-level grades by visiting universities, engineering departments, and conferences.

- Utilization of existing authority – BSEE has actively used existing authority to offer recruitment, retention, and relocation incentives, including student loan repayments, for eligible employees whenever appropriate.

- Partnership - DOI has established a cooperative agreement with the Partnership for Public Service (PPS) to fund Student Ambassadors. Students will be selected competitively from each summer's pool of technical interns to return to their campuses for the new academic year and act as "ambassadors" to DOI to assist in recruitment efforts and branding recognition. BSEE is currently pursuing this partnership and plans to fund two student ambassadors.

Performance Metrics: BSEE measures its Priority Goals by the Number of Employees Age 15-25 (on board) employed by BSEE during the fiscal year.

Administration's Management Agenda
The President's Management Agenda calls for cutting waste and implementing a government that is more responsive and open to the needs of the American people. The Department is actively engaged in supporting this agenda as detailed in "Promoting Efficient Spending Implementation at the Department of the Interior" plan issued December 21, 2011. This implementation strategy outlines some of the ways in

which the Department intends to meet the President's goals in seven key areas. BSEE contributes to the following efforts:

Enterprise Reforms

The Department of the Interior supports the President's Management Agenda to cut waste and implement a government that is more responsive and open. The BSEE budget supports the Department's plan to build upon the Accountable Government Initiative through a set of integrated enterprise reforms designed to support collaborative, evidence-based resource management decisions; efficient Information Technology (IT) Transformation; optimized programs, business processes, and facilities; and a network of innovative cost controlling measures that leverage strategic workforce alignment to realize an effective 21st Century Interior organization.

As outlined in Secretarial Order 3309, the Department of the Interior is taking steps to align IT resources under a single Chief Information Officer (CIO) to minimize redundancies, streamline IT, and enhance customer service, while lowering IT costs to the Department. The subsequent IT Transformation Strategic Plan, which aligns with OMB's 25 Point Implementation Plan to Reform Federal Information Technology Management, outlines high priority IT service areas for immediate modernization. BSEE is committing resources to the planning and implementation of the IT Transformation initiatives for enterprise reforms.

Campaign to Cut Waste

Over the last three years, the Administration has implemented a series of management reforms to curb uncontrolled growth in contract spending, terminate poorly performing information technology projects, deploy state of the art fraud detection tools, focus agency leaders on achieving ambitious improvements in high-priority areas, and open government up to the public to increase accountability and accelerate innovation.

In November 2011, President Obama issued an Executive Order reinforcing these performance and management reforms and the achievement of efficiencies and cost-cutting across the government. This Executive Order identifies specific savings as part of the Administration's Campaign to Cut Waste to achieve a 20 percent reduction in administrative spending from 2010 to 2013 and sustain these savings in 2014. Each agency is directed to establish a plan to reduce the combined costs associated with travel, employee information technology devices, printing, executive fleet services, and extraneous promotional items and other areas.

The Department of the Interior is on target to reduce administrative spending by $217 million from 2010 levels by the end of 2013, and to sustain these savings in 2014. To meet this goal, the Department is leading efforts to reduce waste and create efficiencies by reviewing projected and actual administrative spending to allocate efficiency targets for Bureaus and Departmental Offices to achieve the 20 percent target. Additional details on the Campaign to Cut Waste can be found at http://www.whitehouse.gov/the-press-office/2011/11/09/executive-order-promoting-efficient-spending.

As a new Bureau with planned staffing and resource increases and lacking the clear baseline of a more established Bureau, the focus for BSEE is to establish preliminary targets that reflect a commitment to realizing savings during FY 2013 and sustaining them in FY 2014 wherever possible. BSEE is wholly committed to the Campaign to Cut Waste and will participate fully in the Departmental effort to realizing administrative savings. For example:

- BSEE reduced by $2.5 million its initial estimated need for travel. The target for BSEE is now $4.5 million in lieu of the original $7 million contained in the FY 2013 Budget projection. This decreased baseline figure will be achieved through the increased use of technology, including teleconferencing, video conferences, shared web sites, and web conferences as well as enhanced management attention and internal controls.

- BSEE will achieve savings in transportation of things wherever possible by actively monitoring and controlling relocation spending through examination and update of permanent change of station (PCS) policies, practices, oversight and reporting.

- BSEE supports the Department's goal to reduce spending on advisory and assistance contracts by 20 percent by the end of FY 2013. BSEE will limit its spending for advisory and assistance services and other contractual services by monitoring spending, implementing requirements for justifications and higher-level approvals, designating a central location for justification documentation, and conducting regular review of contracts to identify consolidation opportunities.

- BSEE will achieve savings on supplies and equipment wherever possible by leveraging strategic sourcing contracts and the FedBid Reserve Auction tool for the purchases of commercial products/services.

BSEE is controlling other administrative expenses by initiating internal controls requiring senior-level preapproval of conference-related spending and tracking/reporting funds spent on conferences. Further, BSEE is committed to limiting the publication and printing of hard copy documents in support of more efficient spending practices, while continuing to effectively communicate necessary data for public consumption.

Real Property
In support of the Administration's real property cost savings efforts, the Department issued a policy restricting the maximum amount of Bureau/Office-leased and GSA-provided space to FY 2010 levels and reducing the target utilization rate (square feet per person) for office space by 10 percent. Through actions such as consolidations, collocations, and disposals, BSEE plans to achieve a utilization rate of 180 usable square feet per person by the end of FY 2014 for all new BSEE/BOEM occupancy agreements. BSEE and BOEM efforts to consolidate space will result in achieving a net reduction of over 35,000 rentable square feet.

Data Center Consolidation
The November 2011 Executive Order also asks agencies to "consider the implementation of appropriate agency-wide IT solutions that consolidate activities such as desktop services, email, and collaboration tools." Subsequent OMB budget guidance also directed agencies to reduce Information Technology (IT) spending by ten percent compared with the average spending on IT from FY 2010 to FY 2012. The Department plans to meet both of these charges through its ambitious Information Technology Transformation (ITT) initiative. The ITT will implement a new business model for consolidated delivery of information technology services to Interior's programs and employees and realize both energy and cost savings that can be reinvested in innovative IT solutions that will produce a favorable return on investment.

As part of the Administration's Management Priorities, the Department has initiated a plan for Information Technology (IT) Transformation designed to reduce spending by the consolidation of IT infrastructure and services under a single Chief Information Officer (CIO). The new IT shared services organization will transform the way that IT is delivered to over 70,000 DOI employees, using advances in technology to provide better services for less. BSEE supports the Department's initiative to reduce 95 data centers by FY 2015 without disruption to mission. As part of this initiative, BSEE has initiated a project to reduce its data center footprint and power consumption through the implementation of virtualization in its three primary data center locations: Denver, Herndon, and New Orleans. BSEE plans to reduce the physical size of its Herndon Data Center in FY 2014 by approximately 40 percent and plans a reduction in the size of the Denver Data Center in FY 2016 when the current lease expires. The virtualization project will reduce the number of physical servers to the maximum extent practicable, with the goal of achieving a reduction of 30 percent to 50 percent, which will result in a corresponding reduction in power consumption.

Performance Summary

FY 2014 PERFORMANCE BUDGET
Bureau of Safety and Environmental Enforcement
Strategic Objective Performance Summary

The FY 2014 budget request provides the resources needed to carry out the core functions of the Bureau of Safety and Environmental Enforcement, including offshore regulatory programs; oil spill response planning; safety inspections, enforcement and investigations; environmental enforcement and compliance; well and production permitting; and production and development.

PERFORMANCE MANAGEMENT

The FY 2011 - 2016 DOI Strategic Plan, in compliance with the principles of the Government Performance and Results (GPRA) Modernization Act of 2010, provides a collection of mission objectives, goals, strategies and corresponding metrics that together constitute an integrated and focused approach for tracking performance across the wide range of DOI programs. While the DOI Strategic Plan for FY 2011 – FY 2016 is the foundational structure for the description of program performance measurement and planning for the FY 2014 President's Budget, further details for achieving the Strategic Plan's goals are presented in the DOI Annual Performance Plan and Report (APP&R). Bureau and program specific plans for FY 2014 are fully consistent with the goals, outcomes, and measures described in the FY 2011 - 2016 version of the DOI Strategic Plan and related implementation information in the APP&R.

Within the DOI Strategic Plan for FY 2011 – FY 2016, BSEE is aligned under the second mission area: *Sustainably Manage Energy, Water, and Natural Resources.* Specifically, its functions are captured within Goal One: *Secure America's Energy Resources* and Strategy One: *Ensure environmental compliance and the safety of energy development.* BSEE has two GPRA measures that assess its support of this strategy:

- The *Amount (in barrels) of operational offshore oil spilled per million barrels produced (excluding Hurricane-related spills),* is an annual environmental measure comparing the amount of oil spilled during operations to the amount of oil produced. This measure takes into account all crude oil, condensate, and refined petroleum product spills of one barrel or greater that occur in Federal offshore waters as a result of mineral development, production, and transportation activities on the OCS. Oil spills which occur from acts of nature (e.g., hurricanes and earthquakes), acts of terrorism, or activities other than those involved in Federal OCS oil and gas production and transportation are excluded from the measure (e.g. non-Federal OCS petroleum spills from marine transportation, fishing, recreational and other activities which occurred on the Federal OCS).

- The *Number of Recordable Injuries per 200,000 Offshore Man Hours Worked (100 man years)* is a safety incident rate of all recordable injuries (including fatalities) that are associated with BSEE-regulated activities. Beyond fatalities, recordable injuries are those injuries that require medical treatment beyond first aid, excluding those that are due to natural causes, illness, or that are self-inflicted. The Man Hours Worked count covers all operator and contractor hours worked for production, construction, and drilling operations on the OCS (200,000 man hours equates to approximately 100 full time workers).

BSEE strategies also connect to DOI Mission Area 1: Provide natural and cultural resource protection and experiences; Mission Area 4: Provide a scientific foundation for decision making; and Mission Area 5: Building a 21st century Department of the Interior.

With the development of its new FY 2012-2015 Strategic Plan, BSEE is currently in the process of reviewing and updating its Bureau-level performance measures. BSEE's current GPRA measures, supporting measures, and their respective results are included in the following Goal Performance table.

Table 3: Goal Performance Table

Target Codes:
SP- Strategic Plan measures
HPG- High Performance Goal
BUR - Bureau specific measure
UNK- Prior year data unavailable
TBD- Targets have not yet been developed
NA- Long-term targets are inappropriate to determine at this time

Type Codes: C - Cumulative Measures   A - Annual Measures   F - Future Measures

Mission Area 2: Sustainably Manage Energy, Water, and Natural Resources

Goal 1: Secure America's Energy Resources

Supporting Performance Measures	Type	2008 Actual	2009 Actual	2010 Actual	2011 Actual	2012 Plan	2012 Actual	FY 2013 Plan	FY 2014 President's Budget	Change from 2013 to 2014 Plan	Long-term Target 2016
GPRA Measures											
Amount (in barrels) of operational offshore oil spilled per million barrels produced (excluding Hurricane-related spills) (SP)	A	0 52 (243 8/469 million)	3 9 (2060/531 million)	7,600 (est) (4,590369/ 604 million)	0 42 (est) (243/581 million)	<4 5	0 26 (est) (141/547 million)	<4 5	<4 5	0	<4 5
Total amount (in barrels) of offshore oil spilled per million barrels produced (including Hurricane-related spills) (BUR)	A	12 8 (6007/469 1 million)	3 9 (2060/531 million)	7,600 (est) (4,590369/ 604 million)	0 42 (est) (243/581 million)	--	0 26 (est) (144/547 million)	--	--		--
Contributing Programs	Environmental Enforcement and Operations, Safety and Regulation										
Comments	*In FY 2012, 14 operational spill events greater than 1 barrel were reported resulting in approximately 141 barrels of oil being spilled, with the largest spill reported being approximately 35 barrels. One additional spill of approximately 3 barrels occurred as a result of damage from Hurricane Isaac. Currently production for FY 2012 is estimated to be 547 million barrels resulting in operational and total oil spill ratios of 0.258 and 0.264 respectively. In FY 2010, government scientists estimated that 4.9 million barrels of oil were spilled on the OCS following the explosion and sinking of the Deepwater Horizon drilling rig off the coast of Louisiana. The National Incident Command Report estimated that burning, skimming and direct recovery from the wellhead removed one quarter (25%) of the oil released from the wellhead; one quarter (25%) of the total oil naturally evaporated or dissolved, and just less than one quarter (24%) was dispersed (either naturally or as a result of operations) as microscopic droplets into Gulf waters. Although FY 2010 results for the oil spill ratio greatly exceeded the planned target, future targets will remain at the annual target of less than 4.5 barrels spilled per million barrels produced.* *NOTE: Oil spill data are constantly updated as additional information becomes available through the completion of investigations and/or recovery operations; occasionally, a spill may be deleted or added a year or more later and result in historical data revisions. A final spill volume for the Deepwater Horizon accident has not been determined. Therefore the numerator for the FY2010 Operational Oil Spill ratio and the rate itself are both estimates.*										

Supporting Performance Measures	Type	2008 Actual	2009 Actual	2010 Actual	2011 Actual	2012 Plan	2012 Actual	FY 2013 Plan	FY 2014 President's Budget	Change from 2013 to 2014 Plan	Long-term Target 2016
Number of Recordable Injuries per 200,000 Offshore Man Hours Worked (DOI-Regulated Activities ONLY) (SP)	A	N/A	N/A	N/A	0.30 (revd) (171/569)	<0.63	0.28 (est.) (186/657)	<0.50	<0.50	0	<0.50

Contributing Programs — Operations, Safety and Regulation

Comments: *This strategic plan measure is an incident rate of all Recordable Injuries (i.e., injuries that require medical treatment beyond first aid and fatalities) that occur during DOI-regulated activities in the fiscal year for every 200,000 offshore man hours worked (which is the approximate equivalent of 100 full-time workers). In FY 2012, there were 186 recordable injuries reported for activities with BSEE's jurisdiction and the estimated number of man years worked was 65,761. These estimated results indicate that in FY 2012 there was approximately 1 recordable injury in DOI-regulated activities for every 350 full-time offshore workers. Because safety levels are best evaluated as trends over multiple years, targets for FY 2013 and beyond are based on analysis of historical recordable injury rates against an extrapolation of voluntary man hour reporting from operators in previous years. The Safety and Environmental Management System (SEMS) regulation that went into effect in November 2010 requires all operators to report offshore man hours worked during the calendar year. FY 2012 results will be finalized after BSEE receives calendar year 2012 reporting from operators in March 2013.*

Supporting Performance Measures	Type	2008 Actual	2009 Actual	2010 Actual	2011 Actual	2012 Plan	2012 Actual	FY 2013 Plan	FY 2014 President's Budget	Change from 2013 to 2014 Plan	Long-term Target 2016
Number of fatalities among workers in DOI permitted activities (BUR)	A	2	2	11	2	4	0	3	3	0	Reduce

Contributing Programs — Operations, Safety and Regulation

Comments: *In FY 2012, there were no fatalities among offshore workers in DOI-regulated activities. Because safety levels are best evaluated as trends over multiple years, targets for the fatalities are developed based on reducing a rolling 5-year average, which includes the FY 2010 explosion and sinking of the Deepwater Horizon drilling rig off the coast of Louisiana resulted in 11 deaths.*

Supporting Performance Measures	Type	2008 Actual	2009 Actual	2010 Actual	2011 Actual	2012 Plan	2012 Actual	FY 2013 Plan	FY 2014 President's Budget	Change from 2013 to 2014 Plan	Long-term Target 2016
Less than X% of total gas produced is approved to be flared or vented offshore (BUR) (Calendar Yr)	A	0.51% (11,998,145/ 2,368,336,009 MCF)	0.28% (est.) (5,771,545/ 1,985,369,034 MCF)	0.58% (est.) (9,940,316/ 1,726,885,112 MCF)	0.57% (est.) (7,360,225/ 1,295,657,228 MCF)	0.70%	0.72% (est.) (9,314,529/ 1,298,371,517 MCF)	0.70%	0.70%	0%	TBD

Contributing Program — Environmental Enforcement

Comments: *Industry statistics for venting and flaring show worldwide rates ranging from 0.2% to 100%. Due to satellite monitoring and verification, flaring and venting on the OCS is kept to a minimum. Since FY 2008 U.S. rates have ranged from 0.28% to 0.72%. In April of 2010, BSEE published revised flaring and venting regulations requiring operators to install flare/vent meters on all OCS facilities that process more than 2,000 bbl of oil per day. Previously operators were allowed to estimate these flare/vent volumes. The revised regulations will improve the accuracy of flaring data but may increase reported volumes. Long-term targets will be determined once data has been collected for multiple years under the revised regulations.*

Supporting Performance Measures	Type	2008 Actual	2009 Actual	2010 Actual	2011 Actual	2012 Plan	2012 Actual	FY 2013 Plan	FY 2014 President's Budget	Change from 2013 to 2014 Plan	Long-term Target 2016
Conduct Emerging Technology Research studies on X% of high-priority topics (BUR)	A	93% (14/15)	100% (18/18)	89% (16/18)	94% (15/16)	94%	95% (18/19)	80%	90%	10%	TBD
Contributing Programs	Operations, Safety and Regulation										
Comments	The Emerging Technologies Program (formally known as Technology Assessment and Research (TA&R)) is a research element encompassed within the BSEE Regulatory Program that addresses technological issues associated with energy and mineral operations, ranging from the drilling of oil and gas exploration wells in search of new reserves to the removal of platforms and related infrastructure once production operations have ceased. This metric looks at the percent of studies conducted on high-priority topics. BSEE has implemented a targeted expansion of its technology research following the Deepwater Horizon event to promote and support innovation through the use of Best Available and Safest Technology (BAST) within the drilling, production and response stakeholder communities.										
Achieve a utilization rate of X% at Ohmsett, the national oil spill response test facility (BUR)	A	90% (217/240)	86.2% (207/240)	93% (222/240)	84% (202/240)	85%	94% (226/240)	85%	85%	0%	TBD
Contributing Programs	Oil Spill Research										
Comments	Ohmsett is the National Oil Spill Response Test Facility located in New Jersey. At Ohmsett, clients can test oil spill response equipment in realistic conditions and have training in the use of the equipment. This measure evaluates the utilization level of the facility. The increased focus on oil spill response, as well as expanded uses for the facility such as dispersant training and renewable energy wave tests, have sustained overall utilization rates at around 85%. While the number days Ohmsett will be available in FY 2013 was reduced by Hurricane Sandy, the tank utilization rate of its operational days is not expected to be impacted.										

Supporting Performance Measures	Type	2008 Actual	2009 Actual	2010 Actual	2011 Actual	2012 Plan	2012 Actual	FY 2013 Plan	FY 2014 President's Budget	Change from 2013 to 2014 Plan	Long-term Target 2016
Total Number of Compliance Inspections Completed (BUR)	A	25,650	26,978	23,619	20,537	25,000	23,025	24,000	25,000	1,000	TBD
Contributing Programs	Operations, Safety and Regulation										
Comments	On April 30, 2010, the President directed the Secretary to conduct a 30-day review of the Deepwater Horizon event and to report what additional precautions and technologies should be required to improve the safety of oil and gas exploration and production operations on the outer continental shelf. One of the key recommendations included in that report, as well as other subsequent reports, is that the BSEE needs to increase its oversight and evaluate/ revise the manner in which it conducts its drilling inspections. Since 2010, the inspector/investigator workforce has increased over 40% and BSEE has begun to develop and implement a new inspection strategy that focuses on risk and the use of advanced inspection technologies. Inspection performance trends are not increasing as fast as previously planned due to an increased focus on the witnessing of complex high-risk activities (e.g., BOP testing and cement casing activities) that consume more resources to inspect and the extended time required to hire and train new inspectors so they can independently conduct inspections and other safety/environmental enforcement work. For these reasons, it is difficult to determine how many inspections will be completed beyond FY 2014.										

Supporting Performance Measures	Type	2008 Actual	2009 Actual	2010 Actual	2011 Actual	2012 Plan	2012 Actual	FY 2013 Plan	FY 2014 President's Budget	Change from 2013 to 2014 Plan	Long-term Target 2016
Conduct full Coast Guard inspections on X% of manned offshore facilities annually (BUR)	A	14.7% (164/1112)	13.6% (141/1035) (revd)	16.5% (169/1021)	14.3% (141/985)	10%	14.3% (133/932)	10%	10%	0%	10%
Contributing Programs	Operations, Safety and Regulation										
Comments	*Inspection of U.S. Coast Guard regulated items is a function that was provided for by regulation but one for which BSEE is not reimbursed. Assumption of limited responsibilities by BSEE was pursued following a report by the Inspector General that the U.S. Coast Guard was not conducting inspections of safety items on fixed facilities, as required by law. At this time, BSEE inspectors conduct a limited FPSIP (fixed platform self inspection program) inspection on every platform that they visit and have an annual target of conducting full FPSIP inspections on 10 percent of manned facilities. Although more is done when the resources are available, the targeted percentage of full FPSIP inspections performed by BSEE inspectors has not increased because it would detract from performing inspections of equipment and operations under BSEE jurisdiction.*										

Budget Tables

Bureau of Safety and Environmental Enforcement
Budget at a Glance Table

BSEE Budget-at-a-Glance ($000)						
Account/Activity	FY 2013 Full Year CR	2012 Enacted	Fixed Costs	Internal Transfers	Program Changes	2014 Request
Offshore Safety & Environmental Enforcement (OSEE)						
Environmental Enforcement	*4,117*	4,108	+50	-	+4,156	8,314
Strengthen Environmental Enforcement Program					*[+4,177]*	
Management Efficiencies					*[-21]*	
Operations, Safety and Regulation	*132,306*	132,079	+966	-	+14,237	147,282
Research and Development for Offshore Drilling					*[+2,000]*	
Operational Safety					*[+4,495]*	
National Offshore Training Program					*[+3,685]*	
Wellbore Integrity					*[+1,395]*	
Alaska Program Growth					*[+2,500]*	
Efficiencies in the permitting process: ePermits					*[+1,000]*	
Management Efficiencies					*[-838]*	
Administrative Operations	*15,576*	15,545	+471	-	+3,589	19,605
Sustain Administrative Operations					*[+4,045]*	
Management Efficiencies					*[-456]*	
General Support Services	*12,631*	12,607	+2,690	-	-1,386	13,911
Management Efficiencies					*[-1,386]*	
Executive Direction	*18,202*	18,117	+118	-	-114	18,121
Management Efficiencies					*[-114]*	
Total, OSEE	**182,832**	**182,456**	**+4,295**	**-**	**+20,482**	**207,233**
Offsetting Collections						
Rental Receipts	*-52,587*	-52,587	-	-	+2,019	-50,568
Cost Recovery Fees	*-6,494*	-6,494	-	-	-1,908	-8,402
Inspection Fees	*-62,000*	-62,000	-	-	-3,000	-65,000
Total, Offsetting Collections	**-121,081**	**-121,081**	**-**	**-**	**-2,889**	**-123,970**
Net, OSEE	**61,751**	**61,375**	**+4,295**	**-**	**+17,593**	**83,263**
Oil Spill Research	**14,990**	**14,899**	**-**	**-**		**14,899**
Disaster Relief Appropriations Act, 2013 (P.L. 113-2)	**3,000**	**-**	**-**	**-**	**-**	**-**
Net Appropriations	**79,741**	**76,274**	**+4,295**	**-**	**+17,593**	**98,162**
Total BSEE Funding	**200,822**	**197,355**	**+4,295**	**-**	**+20,482**	**222,132**

This page intentionally left blank.

Bureau of Safety and Environmental Enforcement
Summary of Requirements Tables

Offshore Safety and Environmental Enforcement Appropriation

Summary of Requirements for the Bureau of Safety and Environmental Enforcement
(Dollars in Thousands)

Accounts/Activity	2013 Full Yr. CR (PL 112-175)		2012 Enacted		2014 President's Budget					
	Total FTE	Amount	Total FTE[1]	Amount	Fixed Costs & Related	Internal Transfers	Program Changes	Requested Amount	FTE	FTE Changes [2]
Offshore Safety and Environmental Enforcement										
Environmental Enforcement	18	4,117	7	4,108	+50	-	+4,156	8,314	30	+23
Operations, Safety and Regulation	357	132,306	296	132,079	+966	-	+14,237	147,282	402	+106
Administrative Operations	219	15,576	213	15,545	+471	-	+3,589	19,605	217	+4
General Support Services	0	12,631	0	12,607	+2,690	-	-1,386	13,911	0	+0
Executive Direction	94	18,202	82	18,117	+118	-	-114	18,121	92	+10
Total, OSEE	**688**	**182,832**	**598**	**182,456**	**+4,295**	**-**	**+20,482**	**207,233**	**741**	**+143**
Offsetting Collections										
Rental Receipts	-	-52,587	-	-52,587	-	-	+2,019	-50,568		-
Cost Recovery	-	-6,494	-	-6,494	-	-	-1,908	-8,402		-
Inspection Fees	-	-62,000	-	-62,000	-	-	-3,000	-65,000		-
Total, Offsetting Collections	**-**	**-121,081**		**-121,081**	**-**	**-**	**-2,889**	**-123,970**		**-**
NET TOTAL, OSEE	**688**	**61,751**	**598**	**61,375**	**+4,295**	**-**	**+17,593**	**83,263**	**741**	**+143**

[1] 2012 FTE amounts reflect actual usage, not 2012 enacted formulation estimates

[2] The total FTE increase estimated for FY 2014 is 69 FTE The technical adjustment of 79 FTE represents the difference between 2012 actual and enacted FTE as a result of challenges filling vacant technical positions

Oil Spill Research Appropriation

Summary of Requirements for the Bureau of Safety and Environmental Enforcement
(Dollars in Thousands)

Accounts/Activity	2013 Full Yr. CR (PL 112-175)		2012 Enacted		2014 President's Budget					
	Total FTE	Amount	Total FTE[1]	Amount	Fixed Costs & Related	Internal Transfers	Program Changes	Requested Amount	FTE	FTE Changes [2]
Oil Spill Research	22	14,990	17	14,899	-	-	-	14,899	22	+5
Disaster Relief Appropriations Act, 2013 (P.L. 113-2)	-	3,000	-	-	-	-	-	-	-	-
TOTAL FUNDING, Oil Spill Research	22	17,990	17	14,899	-	-	-	14,899	22	+5

[1] 2012 FTE amounts reflect actual usage, not 2012 enacted formulation estimates

[2] The total FTE increase estimated for FY 2014 is 69 FTE The technical adjustment of 79 FTE represents the difference between 2012 actual and enacted FTE as a result of challenges filling vacant technical positions

This page intentionally left blank.

Bureau of Safety and Environmental Enforcement
Fixed Costs and Internal Realignments

Justification of Fixed Costs and Internal Realignments
(Dollars In Thousands)

Other Fixed Cost Changes and Projections	2012 to 2014 Change
Change in Number of Paid Days	+300
The combined fixed cost estimate includes an adjustment for one additional paid day between FY 2012 and FY 2014.	
Pay Raise	+678
The 2014 Change column relects the total pay raise changes between FY 2012 - FY 2014.	
Employer Share of Federal Health Benefit Plans	+442
The change reflects expected increases in employer's share of Federal Health Benefit Plans.	
Departmental Working Capital Fund	+886
The change reflects expected changes in the charges for centrally billed Department services and other services through the Working Capital Fund. These charges are displayed in the Budget Justification for Department Management.	
Worker's Compensation Payments	+115
The adjustment is for changes in the costs of compensating injured employees and dependents of employees who suffer accidental deaths while on duty. Costs for the BY will reimburse the Department of Labor, Federal Employees Compensation Fund, pursuant to 5 U.S.C. 8147(b) as amended by Public Law 94-273.	
Unemployment Compensation Payments	-7
The adjustment is for projected changes in the costs of unemployment compensation claims to be paid to the Department of Labor, Federal Employees Compensation Account, in the Unemployment Trust Fund, pursuant to Public Law 96-499.	
Rental Payments	+1,881
The adjustment is for changes in the costs payable to General Services Administration (GSA) and others resulting from changes in rates for office and non-office space as estimated by GSA, as well as the rental costs of other currently occupied space. These costs include building security; in the case of GSA space, these are paid to Department of Homeland Security (DHS). Costs of mandatory office relocations, i.e. relocations in cases where due to external events there is no alternative but to vacate the currently occupied space, are also included.	
Total, Fixed Cost Changes	**+4,295**

1/ FY 2012 amounts are not shown because this was the first year of operation for BSEE as a separate bureau

This page intentionally left blank.

Language Citations

Bureau of Safety and Environmental Enforcement
Language Citations

Appropriations Language

Offshore Safety and Environmental Enforcement Appropriation Account

For expenses necessary for the regulation of operations related to leases, easements, rights-of-way and agreements for use for oil and gas, other minerals, energy, and marine-related purposes on the Outer Continental Shelf, as authorized by law; for enforcing and implementing laws and regulations as authorized by law and to the extent provided by Presidential or Secretarial delegation; and for matching grants or cooperative agreements, $142,233,000, of which $83,263,000 is to remain available until September 30, 2015 and of which $58,970,000 is to remain available until expended: Provided, That this total appropriation shall be reduced by amounts collected by the Secretary and credited to this appropriation from additions to receipts resulting from increases to lease rental rates in effect on August 5, 1993, and from cost recovery fees from activities conducted by the Bureau of Safety and Environmental Enforcement pursuant to the Outer Continental Shelf Lands Act, including studies, assessments, analysis, and miscellaneous administrative activities: Provided further, That the sum herein appropriated shall be reduced as such collections are received during the fiscal year, so as to result in a final fiscal year 2014 appropriation estimated at not more than $83,263,000.

For an additional amount, $65,000,000, to remain available until expended, to be reduced by amounts collected by the Secretary and credited to this appropriation, which shall be derived from non-refundable inspection fees collected in fiscal year 2014, as provided in this Act: Provided, That to the extent that amounts realized from such inspection fees exceed $65,000,000, the amounts realized in excess of $65,000,000 shall be credited to this appropriation and remain available until expended: Provided further, That for fiscal year 2014, not less than 50 percent of the inspection fees expended by the Bureau of Safety and Environmental Enforcement will be used to fund personnel and mission-related costs to expand capacity and expedite the orderly development, subject to environmental safeguards, of the Outer Continental Shelf pursuant to the Outer Continental Shelf Lands Act (43 U.S.C. 1331 et seq.), including the review of applications for permits to drill.

Note.--A full-year 2013 appropriation for this account was not enacted at the time the budget was prepared; therefore, the budget assumes this account is operating under the Continuing Appropriations Resolution, 2013 (P.L. 112-175). The amounts included for 2013 reflect the annualized level provided by the continuing resolution.

Justification of Proposed Language Change

Due to issues with the timing difference between collection of rents, cost recovery, and inspection fees and the availability of those amounts for expenditure as offsetting collections, the Department is proposing revised language. The new language is modeled after the Bureau of Land Management (BLM) offsetting collections language in the Management of Lands and Resources Account. The language would derive the funding initially from the general fund of the Treasury with amounts returned to the general fund at the end of the year once all collections have been received.

Oil Spill Research Appropriation Account

For necessary expenses to carry out title I, section 1016, title IV, sections 4202 and 4303, title VII, and title VIII, section 8201 of the Oil Pollution Act of 1990, $14,899,000, which shall be derived from the Oil Spill Liability Trust Fund, to remain available until expended.

Note.—A full-year 2013 appropriation for this account was not enacted at the time the budget was prepared; therefore, the budget assumes this account is operating under the Continuing Appropriations Resolution, 2013 (P.L. 112–175). The amounts included for 2013 reflect the annualized level provided by the continuing resolution as well as amounts from P.L. 113–2, the Disaster Relief Appropriations Act, 2013 (no language shown).

General Provisions

(See General Provision chapter of the Office of the Secretary 2014 budget justification.)

OUTER CONTINENTAL SHELF INSPECTION FEES

SEC. 106. (a) In fiscal year 2014, the Secretary shall collect a nonrefundable inspection fee, which shall be deposited in the "Offshore Safety and Environmental Enforcement" account, from the designated operator for facilities subject to inspection under 43 U.S.C. 1348(c).
(b) Annual fees shall be collected for facilities that are above the waterline, excluding drilling rigs, and are in place at the start of the fiscal year. Fees for fiscal year 2014 shall be:
(1) $10,500 for facilities with no wells, but with processing equipment or gathering lines;
(2) $17,000 for facilities with 1 to 10 wells, with any combination of active or inactive wells; and
(3) $31,500 for facilities with more than 10 wells, with any combination of active or inactive wells.
(c) Fees for drilling rigs shall be assessed for all inspections completed in fiscal year 2014. Fees for fiscal year 2014 shall be:
(1) $30,500 per inspection for rigs operating in water depths of 500 feet or more; and
(2) $16,700 per inspection for rigs operating in water depths of less than 500 feet.
(d) The Secretary shall bill designated operators under subsection (b) within 60 days, with payment required within 30 days of billing. The Secretary shall bill designated operators under subsection (c) within 30 days of the end of the month in which the inspection occurred, with payment required within 30 days of billing.

BUREAU OF OCEAN ENERGY MANAGEMENT, REGULATION AND ENFORCEMENT REORGANIZATION

SEC. 108. The Secretary of the Interior, in order to implement a reorganization of the Bureau of Ocean Energy Management, Regulation and Enforcement, may transfer funds among and between the successor offices and bureaus affected by the reorganization only in conformance with the reprogramming guidelines described in the report accompanying this Act.

SPECIAL PAY AUTHORITY

SEC. 118. The special pay authority provided to the Bureau of Ocean Energy Management and Bureau of Safety and Environmental Enforcement under Section 121(c) of Division E of Public Law 112–74 shall remain in effect for fiscal year2014.

Bureau of Safety and Environmental Enforcement
Proposals for Mandatory Accounts and Offsetting Collections

Federal Oil and Gas Reforms – The Budget includes a package of legislative reforms to bolster and backstop administrative actions being taken to reform the management of DOI's onshore and offshore oil and gas programs, with a key focus on improving the return to taxpayers from the sale of these Federal resources. Proposed statutory and administrative changes fall into three general categories: (1) advancing royalty reforms, (2) encouraging diligent development of oil and gas leases, and (3) improving revenue collection processes. Royalty reforms include: evaluating minimum royalty rates for oil, gas, and similar products; adjusting onshore oil and gas royalty rates; analyzing a price-based tiered royalty rate; and repealing legislatively-mandated royalty relief for "deep gas" wells. Diligent development requirements include shorter primary lease terms, stricter enforcement of lease terms, and monetary incentives to get leases into production. Revenue collection improvements include simplification of the royalty valuation process, elimination of interest accruals on company overpayments of royalties, and permanent repeal of DOI's authority to accept in-kind royalty payments. Collectively, these reforms will generate roughly $2.5 billion in net revenue to the Treasury over ten years, of which about $1.7 billion would result from statutory changes. Many states will also benefit from higher Federal revenue sharing payments.

Transboundary Gulf of Mexico Agreement – The 2014 budget includes a legislative proposal to implement the Agreement between the U.S. and the United Mexican States Concerning Transboundary Hydrocarbon Reservoirs in the Gulf of Mexico, signed by representatives of the U.S. and Mexico on February 20, 2012. The Agreement establishes a framework for the cooperative exploration and development of hydrocarbon resources that cross the United States-Mexico maritime boundary in the Gulf of Mexico through BSEE approved unitization. The Agreement would also end the moratorium on development along the boundary in the Western Gap in the Gulf. The Agreement provides access to an area along the U.S.-Mexico boundary in the Gulf of Mexico roughly the size of Delaware, for exploration and production activities. The area is estimated to contain up to 172 million barrels of oil and 304 billion cubic feet of natural gas. The budget assumes bonus bid revenues from lease sales in this area will generate an estimated $50 million for the Treasury in 2014.

Fee Increase for Offshore Oil and Gas Inspections– Through appropriations language, the Department proposes to increase inspection fees to $65,000,000 in 2014 for offshore oil and gas drilling facilities subject to inspection by BSEE. These fees will support BSEE's expanded inspection program to increase production accountability, human safety, and environmental protection.

This page intentionally left blank.

Environmental Enforcement

FY 2014 PERFORMANCE BUDGET REQUEST
Environmental Enforcement Activity

Table 4: Environmental Enforcement Activity Budget Summary

		2013 *Full Year CR*	2012 Enacted	Fixed Costs (+/-)	Program Changes (+/-)	2014 Budget Request	2014 Changes from 2012 (+/-)
Environmental Enforcement	($000)	*4,117*	4,108	+50	+4,156	8,314	+4,206
	FTE [1]	*18*	7		+23	30	+23

[1] 2012 FTE amounts reflect actual usage, not 2012 enacted formulation estimates.

SUMMARY OF FY 2014 PROGRAM CHANGES

Request Component	Amount ($000)	FTE
Strengthen Environmental Enforcement Program	+4,177	+14
Management Efficiencies	-21	
FTE technical adjustment		+9
Total:	**+4,156**	**+23**

JUSTIFICATION OF FY 2014 PROGRAM CHANGES

The FY 2014 budget request for the Environmental Enforcement Activity is $8,314,000 and 30 FTE, a net program increase of $4,156,000 and 23 FTE over the FY 2012 Enacted level.

Strengthen Environmental Enforcement Program (+$4,177,000; +14 FTE)

The Environmental Enforcement Program was established in FY 2012 to foster environmental compliance, inspection, investigation and enforcement programs that will assure the highest level of environmental standards for all offshore energy activities. Funding provided in that year enabled the hiring of initial personnel necessary to develop and manage the program, and ensure that the NEPA process requirements necessary to responsibly issue permits to conduct various offshore activities were met in each of the OCS regions.

As BSEE enters its third year, the environmental enforcement program is being evaluated as part of an overall enforcement program review. BSEE requests additional base funding to continue implementation of the enforcement program, including the currently identified need of 23 FTE. Resources will be used to:

- Coordinate and target compliance and enforcement actions to address the greatest areas of risk.
- Acquire enhanced data and technology for tracking, verifying and enforcing compliance.

Impacts of Not Funding: BSEE will be unable to provide sufficient integrated Federal oversight of compliance by owners and operators necessary to minimize the safety and environmental impacts of offshore oil and gas development and production operations.

Management Efficiencies (-$21,000): Programs will absorb these costs through greater efficiencies, cost savings, and administrative adjustments.

FTE technical adjustment (+9 FTE)

The technical adjustment of 9 FTE represents the difference between 2012 actual and enacted FTE as a result of challenges filling vacant technical positions. No additional funding is requested/associated with this adjustment.

PROGRAM OVERVIEW

The Program includes the headquarters based Environmental Enforcement Division (EED) and other enforcement coordination activities centered in regional offices. EED is responsible for both the Bureau's own compliance with requirements and the oversight and enforcement of activities by operators on the OCS. These activities include:

- Ensuring BSEE compliance with NEPA and environmental requirements under other statutes and regulations;
- Monitoring industry compliance with mitigation and other environmental requirements; evaluating various environmental mitigation measures to determine their adequacy and appropriately distributing findings; and evaluating, prioritizing, and coordinating potential non-compliance or apparent violations related to environmental requirements;
- Coordinating with BOEM and other Federal, State and local agencies in matters involving environmental compliance and enforcement; and
- Developing new environmental enforcement program activities, including development of appropriate compliance and enforcement targeting tools.

PROGRAM PERFORMANCE

Funding provided in FY 2012 allowed for the timely completion of NEPA review necessary to issue BSEE permits. Based on 2011 data, there are approximately 1,270 NEPA actions, including determinations of NEPA adequacy (DNAs), categorical exclusion reviews (CERs), findings of no significant impact (FONSIs), and environmental assessments (EAs), that the EED is responsible to conduct annually in order to process all of the various BSEE-issued permits without delay.

Though the program's resources have so far been largely dedicated to ensuring the timely processing of BSEE permits, the EED is also establishing procedures and pursuing a small number of environmental violation cases detected since October 1, 2011. These include violations associated with NEPA, Outer Continental Shelf Lands Act, Clean Air Act, Clean Water Act, Endangered Species Act, Marine Mammal Protection Act, Magnuson-Stevens Fishery Conservation and Management Act, and the National Historic Preservation Act.

As stated previously, the environmental enforcement program was created on October 1, 2011; thus, there is no baseline performance data to draw from. Performance measures will be developed for the program once the program's activities, processes, and outcomes are more precisely defined.

Operations, Safety, and Regulation

FY 2014 PERFORMANCE BUDGET REQUEST
Operations, Safety and Regulation Activity

Table 5: Operations, Safety and Regulation Activity Budget Summary

		2013 Full Year CR	2012 Enacted	Fixed Costs (+/-)	Program Changes (+/-)	2014 Budget Request	2014 Changes from 2012 (+/-)
Operations, Safety and Regulation	($000)	132,306	132,079	+966	+14,237	147,282	+15,203
	FTE [1/]	357	296		+106	402	+106

[1/] 2012 FTE amounts reflect actual usage, not 2012 enacted formulation estimates.

SUMMARY OF FY 2014 PROGRAM CHANGES

Request Component	Amount ($000)	FTE
Research and Development for Offshore Drilling	+2,000	0
Operational Safety	+4,495	+33
National Offshore Training Program	+3,685	+7
Wellbore Integrity	+1,395	+9
Alaska Growth Program	+2,500	+6
Efficiencies in the permitting process: ePermits	+1,000	0
Management Efficiencies	-838	0
FTE technical adjustment		+51
Total:	**+14,237**	**+106**

JUSTIFICATION OF FY 2014 PROGRAM CHANGES

The FY 2014 budget request for the Operations, Safety and Regulation Activity is $147,282,000 and 402 FTE, a net program increase of $14,237,000 and 106 FTE over the FY 2012 Enacted.

Research and Development for Offshore Drilling Safety (+$2,000,000; 0 FTE)

BSEE, through its Emerging Technologies Program (formerly the Technology Assessment and Research Program); will use the requested funds for research into important issues that affect the safety and environmental compliance of offshore oil and gas activities. The November 16, 2010, National Academy of Engineering report to Secretary Salazar as well as other reports of findings on the Deepwater Horizon incident have identified a number of procedural and equipment failures that are believed to have contributed to the tragic April 20, 2010, event. These include the lease operator's use of questionable technologies and procedures, lack of effective decision making and lack of understanding of the materials being used. There is an increased need to develop, identify, or assess Best Available and Safest Technologies (BAST), procedures and materials used for offshore oil and gas activities, particularly in deepwater areas, to safeguard human life and the environment. The requested funds will be used to promote identification of and use of BAST associated with energy and mineral operations, ranging from the drilling of oil and gas exploration wells in search of new reserves to the removal of platforms and related infrastructure once production operations have ceased. Although BSEE efforts to advance the technology may involve any aspect of energy and mineral operations, particular attention is given to oil and gas drilling, workover, production, completions, structures, pipelines, decommissioning, human factors/risk assessment, and measurement operations. Under the Emerging Technologies Program, BSEE will use the requested funds to investigate new technologies, procedures and materials that would promote safe operations, the prevention of oil pollution, and the improvement of oil spill response and clean-up.

Starting in FY2012, BSEE focused its funds and efforts to identify high-risk components and systems, such as blowout preventers (BOPs), to ensure that industry was applying BAST in those areas where overall risks could be reduced. To take advantage of and leverage expertise from other Federal resources, BSEE has entered into an Interagency Agreement (IAA) with the Department of Energy National Laboratory System to collaborate on risk-based decision making and applying BAST to offshore components, systems and procedures. The studies from this collaboration are expected to provide BSEE with information to aid current and future inspection workforce and provide regional engineers with the tools to improve the way we assess and approve the use of equipment, procedures and materials. If it is determined that the new component, system, procedures or material is BAST, then BSEE will formalize BAST requirements through NTLs, regulations or conditions of permit, and operators will be required to use equipment that meets the BAST requirements. The requested funds will provide lasting positive impacts on BSEE regulations, Notices to Lessees (NTLs), and industry standards.

Impact of Not Funding: Without this funding, BSEE will experience delays in identifying, assessing, developing, and incorporating new drilling technologies and safety enhancements into agency regulations and operations oversight. Such delays in turn could delay the development of key technological solutions to safely find and develop oil and gas resources under more challenging conditions.

Operational Safety (+$4,495,000; +33 FTE)

In the aftermath of the Macondo well explosion, a multitude of investigations were initiated and their findings discussed in several important reports, most of which came to the same conclusions: that there was an immediate need to improve the safety of offshore operations and to strengthen oil spill response and planning capacity. The rules and regulations of the former MMS has not been able to keep up with the industry's expansion into deepwater drilling— with its larger and more demanding technology, greater pressures and increasing distance from shore-based infrastructure and environmental and safety resources. The agency's ability to develop and maintain up-to-date technical drilling-safety requirements to keep up with industry's rapidly evolving deepwater technology requires staffing increases in key operational areas.

Concurrent with the post-Macondo investigations, DOI developed a three-year plan to identify the resources needed to support the reorganization of the former MMS into three separate agencies, and to implement reforms and increased capacity. The FTEs requested here are consistent with that plan and take into account subsequent recommendations based as presented in the investigatory reports and reorganization study. The requested resources will allow BSEE to:

- develop and implement new performance-based risk assessment and management regulatory programs;

- supplement risk-management programs with rigorous prescriptive safety and pollution-prevention regulations and standards;
- lead the development and adoption of international standards and best practices involving drilling and production;
- provide adequate funding to support safety and environmental oversight, inspection, and enforcement activities; and,
- provide a much better trained response community equipped with better response tools.

This expanded capacity is fundamental to the ability of the Federal government to implement a modern operational safety regime.

Impacts of Not Funding: Without these additional resources, the agency's ability to develop and incorporate new technical requirements, industry standards, and research findings into the regulatory program will be significantly impacted. Furthermore, the ability to ensure that permit applications are processed in a timely manner, inspections are conducted, incidents are thoroughly investigated, and enforcement actions are quickly assessed will be compromised. The proper implementation and enforcement of recently instituted safety initiatives such as the SEMS regulation also will be difficult. Lack of funding and personnel will also significantly impede needed progress on the oil spill program, limiting the Bureau's capacity to review and approve oil spill response plans thoroughly and in a timely manner and hindering the agency's ability to proactively support activities of the National Response System in this post Deepwater Horizon era in which BSEE must take a leadership role in offshore spill planning and preparedness.

National Offshore Training Program (NOTP) (+$3,685,000; +7 FTE)

In FY 2014, BSEE is requesting base funding to support and staff a NOTP to serve as the focal point for continuous learning and training of the Bureau's Safety Inspectors, Environmental Enforcement Officers, and Engineers.

The NOTP supports the Bureau's goals by providing upfront and ongoing contemporary learning and development opportunities to Bureau staff. The NOTP provides a wide variety of recognized and up-to-date training programs. The training will be selected and developed with a focus on the BSEE mission and vision of advancing safety and environmental stewardship principles using the best contemporary science and technology to evaluate, protect, and preserve the human, marine, and coastal environments.

The major goals of the NOTP are as follows:

- To design and deliver programs that recognizes and encourages the continued development of Safety Inspectors, Environmental Enforcement Officers, and Engineers.

- To develop a structured competency-based technical development curricula to meet the needs of a diverse technical audience with an emphasis on BSEE's mission and a focus on safety.

- To build relationships with internal and external stakeholders to ensure the training and educational programs are viewed as a model of efficiency and effectiveness.

In FY 2013 BSEE will continue its efforts to support the expanded oversight role brought about through Bureau reorganization and post-Deepwater Horizon reform measures. This expanded oversight role includes refocusing the existing training program to make better use of the training expertise that is currently being offered by third party organizations. This approach gives the agency the flexibility to quickly adjust the training curriculum to address new technological advances in the industry and to make changes as the needs of the agency staff change.

The benefits of a NOTP are significant. It will allow the agency to develop a more measurable and consistent inspections and compliance program across the organization by increasing employee skills and productivity; reducing attrition through improved job satisfaction; and aiding in the recruiting process. Faced with serious hiring shortfalls, the NOTP will serve as a recruiting tool for future employees seeking additional skills and career guidance.

Impacts of Not Funding: This request establishes initial base funding for the NOTP. Without this funding, BSEE will not be able to enhance its training policy and training programs to maintain and improve the technical and professional capabilities of those employees responsible for ensuring operational safety on offshore facilities. Funding is fundamental to the success of the Bureau and the continued commitment to ensuring safety, environmental protection, and offshore resource conservation through vigorous regulatory oversight and enforcement.

Wellbore Integrity Verification (+$1,395,000; +9 FTE)

Increased safety regulations implemented in November 2010 give BSEE the responsibility to determine whether operators have submitted adequate information demonstrating access and deployment capabilities for surface and subsea containment. Staffing is needed to ensure that BSEE can meet this responsibility, which includes the ability to conduct two new types of evaluations related to wellbore integrity:

1. Determining reservoir fluid gradients - This is a review of all of the sands (gas/oil/water) in a given borehole interval to model the static reservoir fluid gradient for a single sand or a combination of sands. The fluid gradient is then used to determine if the well casing design is adequate or whether the casing will fail causing fluids to breach the borehole and enter the surrounding strata.

2. Determining the consequence of a collapse or burst of the well casing at multiple depths in the well. This second review will indicate the likelihood for the reservoir fluid to be released and reach the sea floor.

These two additional analyses are performed on all Applications for Permit to Drill (APDs) in the GOM that require well containment under the Oil Spill Response regulations. The resulting data will inform continuing regulatory reforms and preserve the Bureau's independence.

Impact of Not Funding: If resources are not sufficient, BSEE cannot ensure that these evaluations will receive an adequate level of technical review or that reviews will be completed in a timely manner to avoid delay of APD approvals. Operators may face delays in the issuance of drilling permits and other important BSEE responsibilities may be deferred as personnel are reassigned to perform this function.

Alaska Program Growth (+$2,500,000; +6 FTE)

The Alaska Region is anticipating significant growth in exploration development, and production activities on the Alaska OCS. The likelihood of success for commercial discoveries is high, and multiple companies have announced their intent to submit applications for drilling. Commercial discoveries would lead to a shift for the Alaska Region from overseeing intermittent exploration and production activities to more intensive development and production activities, including pipeline and production facility design and unitization and reservoir management.

Operators are highly confident their Arctic projects will be a success, and that they will quickly transition into a development process. BSEE expects the need to add additional staff to the Alaska Region to keep pace with the expected development and production engineering functions for platform design, pipelines, unitization, and conservation management. Following a commercial discovery, industry will likely be aggressive in engineering design for development facilities and establishing units for managing reservoir performance and conservation principles. BSEE's Alaska Region will have to perform the review and analysis for all APDs, evaluate technical analysis on calculations and assumptions, and consult supporting maps, diagrams, and studies prior to approval of permits. As future drilling continues, BSEE can expect a proportional increase in the amount of information for review and analysis. Commitments made to provide full-time inspector coverage on active rigs, as well as the logistical difficulties of getting personnel to the Arctic Ocean, will put a significant strain on the existing inspector workforce as the number of activities increase.

This initiative will: 1) build independent and dependable inspection capabilities for significantly expanded drilling activity; 2) build basic engineering support for platform and pipeline functions; 3) build basic engineering and geoscience support for unitization, reservoir and conservation functions; and 4) build administrative support for the increasing volume of administrative files and complex processes.

The inclusion of funding that anticipates the expansion of offshore oil and gas activities in the Arctic is consistent with the Secretary's direction and reinforces the President's commitment to providing careful oversight of future energy development in the Arctic.

Benefits: With this funding support, BSEE's Alaska Region will not be able to provide timely and rigorous technical reviews and inspections of anticipated drilling activities, as well as development and production activities, and to develop and establish precedent setting polices for safe and environmentally protective Arctic development.

Impact of Not Funding: Without this funding, BSEE will not be able to build the technical and administrative support to implement its responsibilities for new development activities in the Arctic. This will inhibit BSEE's ability to provide robust technical review and drilling safety oversight and could lead to delays in permitting future industry operations.

Efficiencies in the permitting process: ePermits (+$1,000,000; 0 FTE)

Technology and information management investments will allow BSEE to better identify trends and statistics critical to assessing the broader indicators of risk, safety, and environmental protection. Additionally, the increased use of data management tools will streamline various Bureau processes such as the submission and review of permits. Based on a recent review, BSEE is finalizing an information management strategic plan and five-year roadmap. BSEE requests additional funding to continue to enhance the management of the permitting process by providing a means for industry to submit permits on-line via the web and to better track the permit review process. To ensure the maximum leveraging of process development, BSEE will partner with BOEM and their ePlans initiative.

ePermits will be a web-based application for receiving and managing all BSEE permits, applications, and reports. In addition to web-based receipt of these documents and data, ePermits will provide the capability to track the evaluation of permits throughout the review process. The use of the ePermit tool will improve the availability and reliability of information needed to make government decisions that ensure compliance with safety and environmental regulations. The tool will also reduce the government time to process permits by replacing manual tasks with automated ones, thus allowing more time to be focused on environmental compliance and safety.

Initial funding will be for the design of the ePermit application and development of the first phases. The ePermit process will provide a web-based process for lease operators to submit drilling, structure, and pipeline permit applications and associated requests and reports to BSEE for approval. In addition to streamlining and providing transparency for the permitting process, ePermits will also link to Pay.gov for fee payment and tracking, thus providing a more efficient means of verifying the receipt of permit application fees.

Benefits:

- An increase in data quality regarding fee payments and links to permits and plans, resulting in a decreased need to issue refunds.

- Provide Industry and the public a more transparent means of understanding and complying with all permitting requirements resulting in faster permit review and approvals.

- Plans and permits will be available in the Electronic Data Management System (EDMS) resulting in:

  o better documentation of the reviews performed for each plan and permit;
  o improved document efficiency for both government agencies and operators; and
  o increased transparency of the permitting process.

Impact of Not Funding: Without this funding request, BSEE's efforts to make the process more efficient and transparent will be further delayed.

Management Efficiencies (-$838,000): Programs will absorb these costs through greater efficiencies, cost savings, and administrative adjustments.

FTE technical adjustment (+51 FTE)

The technical adjustment of 51 FTE represents the difference between 2012 actual and enacted FTE as a result of challenges filling vacant technical positions. No additional funding is requested/associated with this adjustment.

PROGRAM OVERVIEW

BSEE works to assure that energy and mineral development activities are conducted in a safe and environmentally sound manner, with safety being a prerequisite of all activity on the OCS. BSEE continually seeks operational improvements that will reduce the risks to offshore personnel and to the environment, and continually evaluates procedures and regulations to stay abreast of technological advances that will ensure safe and clean operations and conserve the Nation's natural resources. Functions include:

- Regulatory Development
- Standards Development
- Review of OCS Permits
- Inspections, Investigations, and Risk Management
- Safety and Environmental Management
- Operator Performance Reviews

- Civil and Criminal Penalties & Operator Disqualifications
- Real-Time Monitoring
- Conservation Management
- Regulatory Development
- Emerging Technologies
- Oil Spill Response and Planning.

PERFORMANCE OVERVIEW

Regulatory Development: The goal of BSEE's comprehensive management program of energy and mineral operations on the OCS is to ensure that these operations are conducted in a safe and environmentally sound manner. The foundation of this program is a set of regulations that govern all aspects of offshore energy and mineral activities, from engineering specifications for offshore facilities to training requirements for OCS workers. BSEE will continually review these regulations to update and revise them as necessary so that they include the most effective requirements for safety and environmental protection on the OCS. BSEE will continue efforts to improve efficiency in its regulatory program. These efforts will focus on identification and evaluation of regulatory needs; streamlining the regulatory development process to ensure that high quality, enforceable, and legally defensible regulations are generated in a timely manner; streamlining the incorporation of new and updated industry standards into regulations; and effective development and use of guidance documents.

BSEE will continue to develop new regulations and revise existing regulations to ensure safety and environmental protection associated with offshore oil and gas operations. BSEE will focus on regulations related to drilling and production operations, transportation of oil and gas, the use of Best Available and Safest Technology for Blow Out Preventers (BOPs) and the decommissioning of offshore facilities. These regulations will be based on priorities established from a comprehensive review of the existing oil and gas regulations. In addition, BSEE will continue to work with industry groups on standard development and assess those standards for possible incorporation into BSEE's regulations. Regulatory efforts will specifically address oil and gas pipeline requirements for the OCS; production measurement to ensure an accurate assessment of royalties; updates of requirements for decommissioning to ensure that wells and facilities are removed in a timely manner; regulations to address special considerations and best practices for oil and gas development in the Arctic; revisions in regulations to ensure operators use the BAST; and updates to inspection and enforcement provisions to ensure BSEE can use a full range of tools for regulatory compliance.

Standards Development: In FY 2012, BSEE formed and began to staff a new Standards Development Section, under the Regulations and Standards Branch in the Office of Offshore Regulatory Programs in response to recommendations related to the Deepwater Horizon event. This organization actively participates with external Standards Development Organizations (SDOs) to develop new or revised standards for safety and environmental protection on the Outer Continental Shelf (OCS). To minimize travel costs associated with SDO meeting attendance, BSEE located two of the Section staff in Houston, Texas, where most of the SDO meetings are held. This Section assists BSEE by optimizing the use of national and international standards in regulations for safe and environmentally sound development of OCS resources; collaborating with SDOs to expedite the incorporation of industry standards into BSEE regulations; increasing BSEE's knowledge and awareness of standards related to oil and natural gas development on the OCS and their applicability to the regulatory regime; and, facilitating BSEE's ability to provide input on the standards. The new organization has also been tasked with establishing more effective communication links with international standards organizations that can provide additional information to BSEE on the use of BAST standards in international energy development programs.

Review of OCS Permits: Reviews of permits help to ensure that all OCS operators comply with regulatory standards and specific lease stipulations. BSEE performs detailed technical and environmental reviews of plans and permits for exploration, development, and production on OCS lands, as well as permits for other activities such as the installation of pipelines. The ongoing effort by BSEE to develop performance-based operating regulations is expected to generate an increasing number of operator requests for approval of alternative compliance programs. Prior to making approval decisions on alternative compliance, BSEE must assess the alternatives to ensure they provide equal or greater protection than the regulatory requirements they would replace. BSEE will be required to commit a substantial and increasing amount of resources to these assessments in order to evaluate an operator's proposed alternative, verify adherence to approved plans, and determine effectiveness of technologies and procedures employed.

Inspections, Investigations and Risk Management: The OCSLA amendments mandate that annual inspections be performed on each permanent structure and drilling rig that conducts drilling, completion, or workover operations. Safety is a priority for both BSEE staff and for the operations that occur under BSEE jurisdiction, and onsite facility inspections and enforcement actions are important components of BSEE's safety program. The Bureau has established ambitious performance targets for the conduct of thousands of inspections of OCS facilities and operations, including coverage of tens of thousands of safety and pollution prevention components each year to prevent offshore accidents and spills, and to ensure a safe working environment. BSEE's goal is to conduct annual inspections of all oil and gas operations on the OCS to enforce its safety regulations designed to prevent blowouts, fires, spills, and other major accidents. In recent years, BSEE has adopted a goal of conducting monthly inspections of OCS drilling facilities, and therefore providing additional oversight to these specialized facilities. These increases in inspection/oversight, most notably on drilling operations, combined with the increase in OCS oil and gas activities in the Gulf of Mexico, Pacific, and Alaska Regions have required that BSEE increase its inspector workforce and grow their skill base. Additionally, changes in BSEE's inspection philosophy is evolving to promote a focus on the higher risk oil and gas activities in addition to fulfilling the annual inspection requirements mandated in OCSLA amendments.

BSEE is also actively working to develop a risk-based inspection methodology for use at various levels within the regulatory program. The Bureau plans to use the information gleaned from an ongoing risk correlation analysis to learn more about the relative risks posed by discrete offshore oil and gas activities. BSEE will then use the updated risk model to identify and focus Bureau inspections on the "riskiest" activities. Once identified, the Bureau can then hone in on the components used to perform those activities and determine if the relevant Potential Incidence of Non-Compliance (PINCs) and supporting regulations effectively target the risks BSEE would like to guard against. BSEE developed an Interagency Agreement in FY 2012 with Argonne National Laboratory to help develop protocols for a risk-based inspection process for identifying trends in recurring Incidents of Non-Compliance (INCs), defining the inspection elements that correspond to high-risk activities or equipment and identifying potential leading indicators for equipment failures or incidents.

To meet the growing manpower demands, BSEE has engaged in an aggressive hiring effort to ensure its capability to achieve our scheduled and unscheduled inspections. BSEE's inspection workforce has essentially doubled since 2010. This current and anticipated growth in the inspector's ranks will increase the demand and costs associated with our medical standards program for inspectors and inspector training program, both for new hires and refresher training for experienced personnel. In response to this need, BSEE has established a National Offshore Training Program to improve how we provide the inspection workforce with the tools required to successfully perform their inspection duties.

An e-inspection pilot program was launched in selected locations within the Gulf of Mexico Region to test a computer based tool for documenting the inspection process and results. The pilot is being expanded and new capabilities are being considered. BSEE plans to expand the development of additional e-inspections modules to address inspections of fixed platforms as well as for floating rigs.

Additional initiatives were established in 2012 to maintain and improve the efficiencies and effectiveness of the inspection program. In response to growing demands on the aviation resources (e.g., size and number of helicopters necessary to transport our growing inspection workforce) and increase in remote deepwater facilities (i.e., longer travel times), BSEE has recently joined an industry working group to update standards for helideck design for offshore facilities, and is also assessing the availability and placement of offshore refueling facilities. The anticipated decommissioning of the older near-shore offshore facilities and an increase in remote deepwater drilling and production facilities will impact the footprint of available refueling facilities.

During FY 2012 and FY 2013, BSEE started initiatives in risk management to identify leading and lagging indicators to support risk-based inspections and to develop next-generation enforcement tools. BSEE has started collaboration with Argonne National Laboratory to evaluate historic PINCs/INCs to assess patterns that may be a gauge for identifying leading or lagging indicators of safety deficiencies. In addition, BSEE has initiated discussions with the National Aeronautics and Space Administration (NASA) to determine if their existing near-miss database model can be used effectively as a tell-tale of potential risk for the OCS oil and gas industry. BSEE has also held meetings with the Bureau of Transportation Statistics and the International Association of Fire Chiefs, both of which have near-miss reporting programs that have provided them with valuable data on areas of potential risk.

Through these initiatives, BSEE will:

- Study how other regulatory authorities identify and utilize leading/lagging/near miss information and identify best practices.
- Coordinate with other regulators to identify and analyze leading/lagging/near miss information.
- Conduct focused/targeted technical study to identify potential indicators related to high-risk activities (e.g., early kick detection during drilling).
- Conduct studies on best practices for leading/lagging indicators and near misses.
- Work with academia, the private sector and organizations such as NASA to identify and implement a Near Miss Reporting system for the OCS.
- Work with the International Regulators Forum to expand their Performance Indicator Program.
- Review system/component failure information from INCs and other sources to identify applicability to leading/lagging indicators.
- Develop a framework for integrating leading/lagging/near miss information into BSEE risk management activities.

BSEE has the responsibility under OCSLA to conduct investigations and prepare a report of incidents associated with OCS mineral development. The purpose of the investigation is to identify the cause(s) of the incident and to make recommendations to prevent their recurrence and the occurrence of similar incidents. BSEE conducts an initial onsite investigation for many of the incidents reported and reviews all incidents reported to determine whether or not they will be investigated. In FY 2012, 55 incident investigations were conducted. As a result of incident investigation report recommendations and other inspections and enforcement activities, BSEE publishes Safety Alerts to inform the offshore oil and gas industry of the circumstances surrounding an incident or near miss and to provide recommendations that will help prevent the recurrence of a similar incident on the OCS. Incident investigation reports may also recommend that the Bureau consider new or revised regulatory or inspection actions or other initiatives. Through active participation in industry activities such as the American Petroleum Institute's Center for Offshore Safety and aggressively establishing and maintaining relationships with other Government Agencies such as the United States Coast Guard, BSEE promotes effective utilization and coordination of respective investigative resources. Incident investigation reports are published on the BSEE website.

Safety and Environmental Management: The Safety and Environmental Management System (SEMS) is a nontraditional, performance-focused tool for integrating and managing operations on the OCS. All operators on the OCS are required to have a functioning SEMS program in an effort to:

- focus on the influences that human error and poor organization have on accidents;
- seek continuous improvement;
- encourage the use of performance-based operating practices; and
- collaborate with industry in efforts that promote the public interests of offshore worker safety and environmental protection.

According to the current SEMS regulations, all OCS operators must perform their first comprehensive SEMS audit within two years of implementation, i.e. by November 2013. The rule affects lessees and operators of leases and pipeline right-of-way holders on the OCS. This group includes approximately 130 active Federal oil and gas lessees. An estimated 65 percent of these companies are considered small. BSEE is working to provide an effective and comprehensive coverage of this requirement. BSEE must accept and review all audit plans, audit reports, and corrective action plans from approximately 100 operators. This often involves regular correspondence and onsite participation.

BSEE is also involved with several regulatory development initiatives. On December 20, 2012, BSEE published the "Draft Safety Culture Policy Statement" which summarizes the Bureau's expectation that individuals and organizations performing or overseeing activities regulated by BSEE establish and maintain a positive safety culture commensurate with the significance of their activities and the nature and complexity of their organizations and functions. Comments are being accepted through March 2013 and a final policy statement will follow.

BSEE has also revised its original "Safety and Environmental Management" rule and published the new SEMS II rule on April 5, 2013. The SEMS II rule addresses safety concerns that were not covered in the original SEMS rule issued in October 2010. In addition to the current regulatory requirements, operators would be required under the proposed rule to improve the following elements in their SEMS:

- Job Safety Analysis (JSA) – Provide additional requirements for conducting a JSA.
- Auditing - Utilize independent third party auditors to conduct all SEMS audits. The auditors must meet criteria specified in the rule.
- Reporting Unsafe Working Conditions - Empower all facility personnel to report to BSEE possible violations of safety or environmental regulations and requirements and threats of danger.

The SEM II rule includes the following additional SEMS elements:

- Stop Work Authority (SWA) - Creates SWA procedures and authorizes any and all personnel who witness an imminent risk or dangerous activity to stop work.
- Ultimate Work Authority (UWA) - Requires operators to clearly define who has the UWA on the facility for operational safety and decision-making at any given time.

- Employee Participation Plan (EPP) - Provides an environment that promotes participation by employees and management to eliminate or mitigate hazards on the OCS.

Operator Performance Reviews: BSEE conducts Annual Performance Reviews (APR) of each operator. The APR process captures compliance and accident information gathered through the OCS Inspection Program and weighs that information to arrive at a final Operator Performance Index, as well as composite indices that are used as performance indicators for the OCS Regulatory and Compliance program. The Bureau meets with those operators performing at the highest levels to solicit ideas for best operating practices. With the operator's concurrence, BSEE shares these success stories with others through workshops, conferences, and other safety-related meetings. Additionally, BSEE focuses compliance efforts on those operators whose performance does not meet certain targets.

Civil and Criminal Penalties and Operator Disqualification: BSEE, where appropriate, pursues civil and criminal penalty actions against those in violation of Federal regulations, especially when such violations result in, or have the potential to result in, injuries, loss of life, or damage to environmental resources. If an operator exhibits excessively poor, dangerous, or threatening performance, BSEE can assess a civil penalty. BSEE can also issue civil penalties to operators who fail to correct items identified by field inspectors. In calendar year 2012, 31 civil penalty assessments were paid for a total of $2.0 million. BSEE's OCS Civil Penalties Program encourages compliance with OCS statutes and regulations through the pursuit, assessment, and collection of civil penalties (and referrals for the consideration of criminal penalties where warranted). BSEE is committed to strengthening its enforcement programs; this may mean higher civil penalty assessments for poorly performing operators in the future. Should an operator continue to perform poorly, BSEE may place an operator on probation or disqualify a company from operating a specific facility, or all their facilities, on the OCS. The disqualification process provides a structured means to remove operators that pose a threat to the safety of life and the OCS environment.

The cost of administering the Civil Penalties Program is monitored in the Bureau's Activity Based Costing (ABC) system and although the Civil Penalties Program is responsible for less than one percent of Regulatory spending, it is an important enforcement tool on the OCS.

Real-Time Monitoring: The purpose of the Real Time Monitoring (RTM) is to develop, test, and implement reforms that significantly improve the Inspection and Enforcement Program in BSEE by using innovative technologies and using risk-based inspection criteria to supplement BSEE's current inspection program. The use of RTM technology and facilities to monitor OCS oil and gas drilling, well-completion, well workover, well servicing and other rig related operations is one avenue to help meet the BSEE mission. BSEE is also developing a risk-based strategy to determine which available real-time monitoring opportunities would provide the best return on investment and which activities require on-site inspectors. Initially, the focus will be on high-risk activities involving deepwater drilling and casing/cementing. The overall objective is to increase regulatory oversight over critical operations and equipment. The use of real time monitoring will allow BSEE to quickly shift technical resources to evaluate these operations wherever they occur.

As technology advances, RTM is being used more and more by the oil companies, particularly for their higher risk drilling operations such as those in deepwater. This gives companies the opportunity to engage a significantly higher number of experts without the expense of having them actually on the rig or platform. It also allows operators to use expert advisors to participate in an advisory capacity; to provide the offshore drilling personnel with "a second set of eyes." Providing BSEE technical experts' access to this information during high-risk activities would also give BSEE access to their on-shore experts, allowing real-time queries into the decision processes as activities progress.

To evaluate the current state of monitoring technology, BSEE sent technical engineering staff to review the activities in three RTM centers to determine which of these real-time monitoring capabilities could feasibly be incorporated into BSEE's regulatory regime and inspection program. BSEE took the available information gathered during these meetings and in FY 2012 contracted for an independent assessment of the various types of real-time data monitoring systems available for offshore oil and gas operations. The assessment will focus on drilling and production technologies and include a cost benefit analysis that would detail potential costs to industry; potential increases in safety performance; government resources needed for implementation; and necessary training for all parties involved. The assessment will identify what automation systems are available or being developed, the potential they have to increase offshore drilling safety, and any negative impacts they have on operations. The final report is due in August, 2013.

In FY 2012, BSEE also ran ground truth tests in two OCS Regions to determine the effectiveness of RTM for Blowout Preventer (BOP) witnessing. BSEE placed personnel on-site as well as in on-shore offices reviewing real-time data streaming. In these tests, inspectors found that, with the current technology, on-site witnessing appeared to have greater benefits than RTM. However, it was also indicated that RTM of the data could be a substitute if offshore trips were precluded by weather or other circumstances. Additional investigations are being planned to determine if additional training or improvements in technology in RTM evaluations could improve the benefits of onshore RTM.

As part of the BSEE 2015 Strategic Plan Initiative that was developed in FY 2012 and is being implemented in FY 2013, the agency is placing increased emphasis on evaluating and initiating real-time monitoring and risk-based inspection strategies. Some of the planned activities include collaboration and use of the Department of Energy's National Laboratory System. These proposed studies include:

- Real time early kick detection at the drill bit using routine attenuated acoustic data.
- Intelligent Casing/Intelligent Telemetry. Exploring the feasibility of increasing bandwidth for smart pipe that will allow better real-time determination of down-hole conditions.
- Identification of a multi-layered, real-time monitoring system to allow automated well control and maintenance of down-hole well conditions with data transfer capabilities for real-time kick detection.
- Identification of leading indicators that either should be monitored in real time or need to have real time monitoring protocols developed to decrease the risk of drilling operations.

BSEE is also investigating the potential use and costs of using unmanned aerial systems and satellites to enhance RTM efforts for inspection, enforcement, and damage assessment. Aircraft and satellites can provide images and data for a wide range of BSEE missions, such as spotting pollution; monitoring for illegal venting or flaring activity; conducting post-hurricane damage assessments; monitoring for marine mammals; and enforcing lease/permit stipulations. One possible RTM application is to use Unmanned Aircraft Systems (UASs) to monitor drilling and production operations, such as monitoring pipeline routes in the Arctic and thereby eliminate the risk to personnel of having to fly offshore in this remote and hostile environment. The Federal government, NASA, and the private sector have UAS technology that could meet BSEE's needs for integrating RTM into BSEE's safety and enforcement mission. Evaluations are being conducted on the possible sensor packages that could be available and an analysis of the cost-benefit is being developed.

Access to relevant real-time data and the ability to visualize the data could be a valuable tool in BSEE's inspection program. BSEE is currently evaluating how to phase in available RTM technology and stay abreast of emerging RTM technology. BSEE will be:

- Focusing its regulatory oversight on the most significant data by collaborating with international regulators and the industry to identify leading and lagging indicators that can be used, along with appropriate models, to predict unsafe conditions based on real-time data.
- Evaluating the cost of advanced RTM technology and how to prioritize RTM requirements and incorporate some of the higher risk and larger deepwater activities.
- Identifying and defining the type of data that operators must collect and analyze and assessing which regulations would need to be modified to allow BSEE to use RTM technology to enhance its inspection capabilities.
- Ascertaining the necessary training that BSEE engineers and inspectors will need to attain the different skill sets for applying RTM to our inspection and oversight programs.

Conservation Management: As a steward of the Nation's OCS mineral resources, BSEE must provide for conservation of natural resources by preventing waste and ensuring ultimate recovery of the resources, as well as protecting the correlative rights of OCS lessees and the government. Conservation of oil and gas resources is an integral part of the Nation's energy policy and a primary objective for the BSEE regulatory program. To promote conservation, BSEE monitors development and production activities on the OCS and enforces regulations that require operators to avoid waste and maximize the ultimate recovery of OCS minerals once access has been granted.

In FY 2013, BSEE initiated a detailed field study for the Point Arguello Field offshore California using all relevant data, including seismic surveys; well logs and well files drilling and development histories; existing literature; and production histories. The study will provide BSEE with information on the reserves estimates using volumetric calculations and analysis of production performance history. The study will also yield an assessment of the reserves that are economically recoverable under existing economic conditions and also provide an estimate of reserves if the economic conditions improve significantly (e.g., 50 percent increase in oil price). The study will also determine if there are any incremental reserves that can be gained by drilling additional wells/sidetracks, using enhanced recovery techniques, and identifying wells that could be used for water and/or gas injection, if applicable.

BSEE is encouraged that this study will help define a template for additional studies of reservoir dynamics that will allow BSEE to fulfill its responsibilities under OCSLA to maximize the production of U.S. owned oil and gas resources from end-of-life reservoirs and serve as a model for mid-life and end-of-life reservoir analyses.

Emerging Technologies (formerly Technology Assessment and Research): BSEE continues to promote identification of and use of BAST associated with energy and mineral operations, ranging from the drilling of oil and gas exploration wells in search of new reserves to the removal of platforms and related infrastructure once production operations have ceased. Although BSEE efforts to advance the technology may involve any aspect of energy and mineral operations, particular attention is given to oil and gas drilling; workover; production; completions; structures; pipelines; decommissioning; human factors/risk assessment; and measurement operations. Under the Emerging Technologies program, BSEE furthers the investigation of new technologies to promote safe, pollution-free operations and prevention of oil pollution and the improvement of oil spill response and clean-up.

Starting in FY 2012, BSEE focused its efforts to identify high-risk components and systems, such as blowout preventers BOPs, to ensure that industry was applying BAST in those areas where overall risks could be reduced. To take advantage of and leverage expertise from other Federal resources, BSEE has entered into an Interagency Agreement (IAA) with the Department of Energy's National Laboratory System to collaborate on risk-based decision making and applying BAST to offshore components, systems and procedures. The studies from this collaboration are expected to provide BSEE with information to aid the current and future inspection workforce and provide regional engineers with the tools to improve the way the use of BOPs are assessed and approved since these devices are considered to be the last line of defense for well containment. These studies and other 2012 and 2013 studies will provide lasting impacts on BSEE regulations, Notices to Lessees (NTLs), and industry standards.

BSEE has also developed BAST protocols that are being implemented and will be used to focus its funding resources on the most beneficial BAST opportunities. This includes the establishment of a technical panel comprising outside experts that will evaluate potential BAST, work with standards organizations/industry to develop testing protocols for technologies, identify accredited laboratories to perform required testing and generate a test and evaluation plan for the Director of BSEE. For those technologies that are determined sufficient and economically feasible, BSEE will move them into a testing phase using accredited test laboratories under the supervision of the technical panel and BSEE.

If it is determined that the new component, system or procedures are BAST, then BSEE will formalize BAST requirements through NTLs, regulations, or conditions of permits, and operators will be required to use equipment that meets the BAST requirements.

BSEE has also contracted with the National Academy of Sciences (NAS), which has formed a committee to identify options that BSEE could use for improving the implementation of the BAST requirement in the OCSLA. The NAS committee will review various options including the feasibility and appropriateness of establishing a formal industry committee to make BAST determinations about new and improved technologies; whether BSEE will need to develop test protocols for every technology it evaluates in order to fairly compare competing technologies; how to determine economic feasibility in a manner that is independent of industry; whether BSEE should rely on the development of consensus standards; and whether BSEE should initiate a more vigorous process with various possible improvements to blowout preventers. The committee will include consideration of the following in its report:

- Other relevant safety requirements that bear upon technologies for offshore oil and gas operations;
- Relevant reports of previous National Response Center (NRC) committees and other organizations;
- The potential role of neutral third parties in making BAST assessments;
- The role of human factors in the safe use of technologies by industry; and
- Resource requirements of Federal agencies for BAST implementation.

BSEE continues to actively seek opportunities for joint projects to leverage available funds and disseminate research findings. Participation in jointly funded projects with industry, other Federal and state agencies, academia, and international regulatory organizations has become an important mechanism for BSEE to improve its understanding of important safety issues. In 2012, BSEE participated in 14 joint projects and plans to continue to seek opportunities to leverage available funds through joint projects with other organizations.

Oil Spill Response and Planning: The Oil Spill Response Division (OSRD) has the responsibility for ensuring that the offshore operators and response community have the necessary equipment, resources, trained personnel, and established plans to carry out an effective, efficient response to a worst case discharge from an offshore source. Division staff fully integrates into activities of the National Response System through appointment to positions on the National Response Team Preparedness Subcommittee, and Scientific and Technical Committee, Regional Response Teams affecting policy for the Gulf of Mexico, Pacific, and Alaska Regions, and applicable Area Committees.

The OSRD compliance staff (10 FTE nationally), provides continuous Federal oversight that requires reoccurring compliance actions during the entire lifecycle of offshore oil and gas facilities, from drilling a well to decommissioning and removal. OSRD conducts over 160 plan reviews a year which are required to maintain oversight responsibilities for the nearly 200 approved Oil Spill Response Plans (OSRPs) as operators maintain or revise their content. OSRD staff also conducts equipment validation inspections at over 60 locations, attend 35 industry led exercises, and initiate 25 unannounced government led exercises each year to validate readiness nationwide. OSRD is also developing procedures to move toward a more proactive enforcement program that will require daily monitoring, tracking, and investigation into approximately 4,000 self-reported offshore spills a year to ensure operator compliance.

Internal and external coordination is imperative to strengthening the Nation's readiness for an oil spill. BSEE collaborates with other Federal and State response agencies when reviewing oil spill response plans. BSEE also collaborates with international partners. Internally, OSRD is working with other BSEE divisions to proactively identify spills that were not reported to take enforcement actions for notification violations. During responses to incidents offshore, BSEE supports all levels of response organizations as subject matter experts in offshore oil spill response.

Work will continue to improve preparedness as OSRD develops oil spill plan regulatory revisions. The recent completion of a joint BSEE and United States Coast Guard (USCG) project to develop new national response planning standards will influence both agencies' regulations. Coordination with the USCG will continue through the Response Workgroup on projects involving a national response resource database, an update to the National Preparedness for Response and Exercise Program (NPREP), Area Contingency Plan revisions through chairing the offshore Worst Case Discharge (WCD) sub teams of each Area Committee, drill coordination, and other activities to enhance spill preparedness. BSEE will continue to respond to recommendations from the Incident Specific Preparedness Review and similar response-focused reports to ensure that lessons learned are fully implemented to improve overall operations.

BSEE will continue to support the Federal On-Scene Coordinator (FOSC) during a spill response with subject matter expertise to the Incident Command System structure for offshore drilling and source control. Activities during the Macondo well blowout revealed the critical skill sets that BSEE staff possesses in well completion and design and their value in well containment and relief well operations. OSRD staff will deploy to incident command posts to provide expert assistance to the FOSC on offshore operations and to coordinate the deployment of BSEE engineering, technical, and/or scientific staff to support spill abatement and response activities for spills originating from facilities under the jurisdiction of BSEE.

Table 9: Performance Overview Table- Operations, Safety and Regulation

Supporting Performance Measures	Type	2008 Actual	2009 Actual	2010 Actual	2011 Actual	2012 Plan	2012 Actual	FY 2013 Plan	FY 2014 President's Budget	Change from 2013 to 2014 Plan	Long-term Target 2016
Number of Recordable Injuries per 200,000 Offshore Man Hours Worked (DOI-Regulated Activities ONLY) (SP)	A	N/A	N/A	N/A	0.30 (revd) (171/569)	<0.63	0.28 (est) (186/657)	<0.50	<0.50	0	<0.50
Contributing Programs	Operations, Safety and Regulation										
Comments	*This strategic plan measure is an incident rate of all Recordable Injuries (i.e., injuries that require medical treatment beyond first aid and fatalities) that occur during DOI-regulated activities in the fiscal year for every 200,000 offshore man hours worked (which is the approximate equivalent of 100 full-time workers). In FY 2012, there were 186 recordable injuries reported for activities with BSEE's jurisdiction and the estimated number of man years worked was 65,761. These estimated results indicate that in FY 2012 there was approximately 1 recordable injury in DOI-regulated activities for every 350 full-time offshore workers. Because safety levels are best evaluated as trends over multiple years, targets for FY 2013 and beyond are based on analysis of historical recordable injury rates against an extrapolation of voluntary man hour reporting from operators in previous years. The Safety and Environmental Management System (SEMS) regulation that went into effect in November 2010 requires all operators to report offshore man hours worked during the calendar year. FY 2012 results will be finalized after BSEE receives calendar year 2012 reporting from operators in March 2013.*										
Number of fatalities among workers in DOI permitted activities (BUR)	A	2	2	11	2	4	0	3	3	0	Reduce
Contributing Programs	Operations, Safety and Regulation										
Comments	*In FY 2012, there were no fatalities among offshore workers in DOI-regulated activities. Because safety levels are best evaluated as trends over multiple years, targets for the fatalities are developed based on reducing a rolling 5-year average, which includes the FY 2010 explosion and sinking of the Deepwater Horizon drilling rig off the coast of Louisiana resulted in 11 deaths.*										
Conduct Emerging Technology Research studies on X% of high-priority topics (BUR)	A	93% (14/15)	100% (18/18)	89% (16/18)	94% (15/16)	94%	95% (18/19)	80%	90%	10%	TBD
Contributing Programs	Operations, Safety and Regulation										
Comments	*The Emerging Technologies Program (formally known as Technology Assessment and Research (TA&R)) is a research element encompassed within the BSEE Regulatory Program that addresses technological issues associated with energy and mineral operations, ranging from the drilling of oil and gas exploration wells in search of new reserves to the removal of platforms and related infrastructure once production operations have ceased. This metric looks at the percent of studies conducted on high-priority topics. BSEE has implemented a targeted expansion of its technology research following the Deepwater Horizon event to promote and support innovation through the use of Best Available and Safest Technology (BAST) within the drilling, production and response stakeholder communities.*										

Supporting Performance Measures	Type	2008 Actual	2009 Actual	2010 Actual	2011 Actual	2012 Plan	2012 Actual	FY 2013 Plan	FY 2014 President's Budget	Change from 2013 to 2014 Plan	Long-term Target 2016
Total Number of Compliance Inspections Completed (BUR)	A	25,650	26,978	23,619	20,537	25,000	23,025	24,000	25,000	1,000	TBD

Contributing Programs Operations, Safety and Regulation

Comments

On April 30, 2010, the President directed the Secretary to conduct a 30-day review of the Deepwater Horizon event and to report what additional precautions and technologies should be required to improve the safety of oil and gas exploration and production operations on the outer continental shelf. One of the key recommendations included in that report, as well as other subsequent reports, is that the BSEE needs to increase its oversight and evaluate/ revise the manner in which it conducts its drilling inspections.

Since 2010, the inspector/investigator workforce has increased over 40% and BSEE has begun to develop and implement a new inspection strategy that focuses on risk and the use of advanced inspection technologies. Inspection performance trends are not increasing as fast as previously planned due to an increased focus on the witnessing of complex high-risk activities (e.g., BOP testing and cement casing activities) that consume more resources to inspect and the extended time required to hire and train new inspectors so they can independently conduct inspections and other safety/environmental enforcement work. For these reasons, it is difficult to determine how many inspections will be completed beyond FY 2014.

Supporting Performance Measures	Type	2008 Actual	2009 Actual	2010 Actual	2011 Actual	2012 Plan	2012 Actual	FY 2013 Plan	FY 2014 President's Budget	Change from 2013 to 2014 Plan	Long-term Target 2016
Conduct full Coast Guard inspections on X% of manned offshore facilities annually (BUR)	A	14.7% (164/1112)	13.6% (141/1035) (revd)	16.5% (169/1021)	14.3% (141/985)	10%	14.3% (133/932)	10%	10%	0%	10%

Contributing Programs Operations, Safety and Regulation

Comments

Inspection of U.S. Coast Guard regulated items is a function that was provided for by regulation but one for which BSEE is not reimbursed. Assumption of limited responsibilities by BSEE was pursued following a report by the Inspector General that the U.S. Coast Guard was not conducting inspections of safety items on fixed facilities, as required by law. At this time, BSEE inspectors conduct a limited FPSIP (fixed platform self inspection program) inspection on every platform that they visit and have an annual target of conducting full FPSIP inspections on 10 percent of manned facilities. Although more is done when the resources are available, the targeted percentage of full FPSIP inspections performed by BSEE inspectors has not increased because it would detract from performing inspections of equipment and operations under BSEE jurisdiction.

This page intentionally left blank.

Administrative Operations

FY 2014 PERFORMANCE BUDGET REQUEST
Administrative Operations Activity

Table 10: Administrative Operations Activity Budget Summary

		2013 *Full Year CR*	2012 Enacted	Fixed Costs (+/-)	Program Changes (+/-)	2014 Budget Request	2014 Changes from 2012 (+/-)
Administrative Operations	($000)	*15,576*	15,545	+471	+3,589	19,605	+4,060
	FTE [1]	*219*	213		+4	217	+4

[1] 2012 FTE amounts reflect actual usage, not 2012 enacted formulation estimates.

SUMMARY OF FY 2014 PROGRAM CHANGES

Request Component	Amount ($000)	FTE
Sustain Administrative Operations	+4,045	0
Management Efficiencies	-456	
FTE technical adjustment		+4
Total:	**+3,589**	**+4**

JUSTIFICATION OF FY 2014 PROGRAM CHANGES

The FY 2014 budget request for the Administrative Operations Activity is $19,605,000 and 217 FTE, a net program increase of $3,589,000 and 4 FTE from the FY 2012 Enacted.

Sustain Administrative Operations (+$4,045,000; 0 FTE)

Prior to the reorganization of the former MMS, funding provided through the Administrative Operations activity supported more than 1,700 FTEs in three major program areas – Minerals Revenue Management, Offshore Energy Minerals Management, and General Administration.

This funding provided the ability to provide a full suite of services, including general administration, ethics, equal employment opportunity, emergency management, finance, human resources, procurement, and information management.

The reorganization and reform efforts begun in FY 2011, and continuing into FY 2012 and FY 2013, have successfully changed the organizational structure, its processes, and supporting financial practices. It has also required new budget structures with new appropriations and activities, and the need to develop new accounting nomenclatures. Although more than 600 positions were transferred, along with administrative support funding to ONRR, the projected FTEs for BOEM and BSEE are expected to increase to more than 1,300.

BSEE is requesting $4,045,000 to sustain the necessary level of support services for these organizations. This is a request to adjust the base to provide sufficient administrative services to support the BSEE and BOEM workforce. Before making this request, opportunities to be more efficient and to minimize costs were studied. Through this review, BSEE determined additional funds are needed to address the demands of servicing two organizations that are projected to grow.

The funding will be used to retain the expertise and personnel that will serve BOEM and BSEE as the Bureaus recruit new inspectors, engineers, and scientists and conduct additional environmental and technological studies. It will support BSEE's ability to advertise critical vacancies for inspectors, engineers, and other professionals in a timely manner. Many of these actions are time-consuming and involve multiple grade levels, and numerous personnel actions are needed when advertising both within and outside the Federal government. Similarly, in the acquisition services area, funding support will enable BSEE to continue the procurement of mission-critical environmental and engineering studies in a timely manner.

Impacts of Not Funding: Without a funding adjustment, both Bureaus are likely to encounter delays in filling critical vacancies and in supporting our program personnel appropriately. This often results in the best candidates finding other employment during the prolonged recruitment process. Procurement lead-time required for complex contracts could increase by 35 percent, delaying the Bureaus' ability to perform mission critical work, while the lead-time for smaller procurement actions could increase by 50 – 100 percent.

Financial services could be compromised as well, increasing the processing time for financial transactions, including the processing of vouchers and invoices that will delay the completion of environmental and engineering studies, the performance of offshore facility inspections, and other mission critical functions. The requested funding for these administrative activities is imperative to support the mission of these new organizations.

Management Efficiencies (-$456,000): Programs will absorb these costs through greater efficiencies, cost savings, and administrative adjustments.

FTE technical adjustment (+4 FTE)

The technical adjustment of 4 FTE represents the difference between 2012 actual and enacted FTE as a result of challenges filling vacant technical positions. No additional funding is requested/associated with this adjustment.

PROGRAM OVERVIEW

The Administrative Operations Activity consists of the following functions: Administrative Direction and Coordination, Finance, Equal Employment Opportunity, Human Resources, Acquisition Management, and Information Management.

Acquisition Management Division: The Acquisition Management Division is responsible for the execution and administration of BSEE and BOEM contracts and financial assistance agreements. By collaborating with the customer organizations, they create quality business solutions that help to accomplish the mission goals of the Bureaus. The Division provides acquisition and financial assistance policy guidance, cost and price analysis, and advice to procurement and program personnel. They conduct acquisition management and other internal control reviews of procurement activities. They also administer the purchase line of the BSEE and BOEM charge card programs as well as their competitive sourcing programs. In addition, they manage the Business and Economic Development Program to maximize opportunities for small, disadvantaged, and women-owned businesses, as well as historically black colleges and universities as both prime contractors and subcontractors. They also oversee all acquisition career management programs.

Equal Employment Opportunity Division (EEOD): The EEOD develops, monitors, and operates the Equal Employment Opportunity (EEO) program for BSEE and BOEM in compliance with the Civil Rights Act of 1964, the Equal Employment Opportunity Act of 1972, Executive Order 11478, departmental directives, and other related statutes and orders. Its goal is to ensure that workforce activities are inclusive, that they promote the full utilization and exchange of skills and talents.

The Division provides advice and guidance to managers, supervisors, and employees regarding EEO policies and procedures. EEOD provides technical advice and consultation to managers on recruitment strategies for affirmative employment designed to improve low participation rates of various groups in BSEE and BOEM. EEOD provides oversight of special initiative programs designed to involve more women, minorities, and people with disabilities throughout all levels of management. The Division also provides an alternative dispute resolution program, counseling and mediation services, as well as formal EEO complaint processing.

Finance Division: The Finance Division (FD) provides a full range of accounting and financial management services to BSEE and BOEM. The FD manages and oversees the Bureau-level CFO related audit as conducted by an independent audit firm with oversight from the Department's Office of Inspector General (OIG). The FD develops Bureau financial policies, procedures, and guidelines. The Division maintains liaison with departmental policy offices, including the Office of Financial Management and the Office of Acquisition and Property Management. It also coordinates with the Bureau Office of Budget and with the Department's Office of Budget. Staff members may also represent the Bureau on a variety of departmental and government-wide teams dealing with financial issues.

This Division is responsible for the administrative accounting operations of both BSEE and BOEM. The FD manages the administrative accounting system; audits and schedules bills for payments; collects debts; develops financial data; prepares financial reports; provides advice and guidance on financial matters; and maintains liaison with departmental offices and other Federal agencies.

Human Resources Division: The Human Resources (HR) Division develops and implements policies, procedures, guidelines, and standards relating to general personnel management, recruitment and employment, position management and classification, and employee development. Work includes performing all operational personnel services for BSEE and client organizations, and providing assistance and guidance related to personnel matters for all regional and field installations.

The HR Division also leads all BSEE and BOEM workforce-planning initiatives, which include analyzing the current workforce, identifying future workforce needs, and preparing plans for building the workforce needed in the future. The long-term benefits of workforce-planning initiatives include the ability of BSEE and BOEM to meet their mission and performance goals. As regulators, BSEE must be able to keep pace with the latest technological advances. In support of these efforts, the Division works with its customers to adopt a comprehensive recruitment and training system in order to attract the best talent to the public service while continuing to provide the training and education necessary to keep its workforce at the leading edge of industry innovation.

The Division focuses on employee relations and services, including personnel program evaluation, labor/management relations, advising employees about conflict of financial interest and standards of conduct, and administering incentive awards programs, family friendly programs, the Federal Equal Opportunity Recruitment Program, and Senior Executive Service program. In addition, the Division is responsible for the development of training policy and oversight of a Bureau-wide Learning Management System that will serve as a valuable workforce planning and management tool. The HR Division also coordinates all departmental mandated employee development initiatives for implementation in BSEE and BOEM.

Technology Services Division: The Technology Services Division (TSD) ensures the efficient and effective planning, management and acquisition of information technology and information resources within BSEE, BOEM, and ONRR and ensures compliance with all DOI and Federal information resources management policies and guidelines. In alignment with the Department's IT Transformation, the Division clearly distinguishes the information technology needs of the Bureau's mission and enterprise functions.

The TSD provides a central foundation to manage the large volume of information and data used in the scientific, engineering, and management activities of the BSEE and BOEM programs. At the core of the IT capabilities is the Technical Information Management System (TIMS). TIMS automates the business and regulatory functions of BSEE and BOEM and brings diverse information into a central database. This enables BSEE and BOEM Regions and Headquarters to share and combine data; to standardize processes, forms, reports, and maps; to promote the electronic submission of data; to enforce data integrity through relational database technology; and to release accurate, consistent information to the public sector.

In support of the strategic goals of the Bureau, TSD through a collaborative effort with its customer base will redesign its information and knowledge management tools, and enhance the collection, standardization, accuracy, completeness, consistency, and storage of data. These efforts will increase the Bureau's ability to collaborate across current divisions of process and software. Improved data management and analysis will allow the Bureau to better identify trends and statistics critical to assessing broader indicators of risk. A more collaborative and streamlined knowledge management system will also better enable agency-wide innovation and adaptation in all aspects of offshore safety, response preparedness, and environmental protection.

The TSD also manages and maintains the Geological Interpretive Tools (GIT) system, which represents the basis of essentially all BOEM determinations requiring geoscience analysis. GIT allows BOEM to improve productivity by quantifying analyses, analyzing digital data in three-dimensions (3-D), fully integrating geophysical and geological data analysis, and reducing risks and uncertainty in decision-making processes. In addition, TSD has developed an extensive Geographic Information System (GIS) capability for nearly all BSEE and BOEM offshore maps and leasing processes, providing us the means to define, describe, analyze, and account for every acre of Federal offshore-submerged lands.

The Division provides direction and coordination for Bureau-wide IT activities such as the IT Capital/Strategic Planning, with an emphasis on IT investment planning and monitoring through a vigorous governance process. They also provide support for the overall infrastructure, including the shared services budget, enterprise help desk, network management, and other essential infrastructure for office automation. The TSD implements and supports the Bureau's IT security program by working collaboratively with the BSEE and BOEM offices as well as with the DOI's Office of the CIO to review and improve security plans, policies, procedures, and standards to reflect technological changes. The IT security efforts include participating in risk assessments and management reviews of systems and networks, identifying security issues, and recommending mitigation.

Management Support Division: The Management Support Division (MSD) provides direct assistance to BSEE's Associate Director for Administration, as well as to BSEE and BOEM personnel. MSD's responsibilities include:

- Emergency management, physical security, personnel security;
- Evaluations and studies;
- Delegation of authority, directives management, program management, providing high-level administrative support; and management and organization analysis activities;
- Occupational safety and health;
- Support services, including facilities management, property management, space management, printing and publications activity, and general office services;
- Continuity of operations program; plans, implements, and directs the physical and personnel security programs, including development and implementation of policy, procedures, methods, and techniques for protection of proprietary and national security information;
- Budget planning, execution, and formulation for the administrative operations and the general support services budgets;
- Maintains accountability records of all system-controlled property in the possession and control of custodial property officers and contractors and manages the vehicle fleet and the museum property, including an Arts and Artifacts program.

This page intentionally left blank.

General Support Services

FY 2014 PERFORMANCE BUDGET REQUEST
General Support Services Activity

Table 11: General Support Services Budget Summary

		2013 *Full Year CR*	2012 Enacted	Fixed Costs (+/-)	Program Changes (+/-)	2014 Budget Request	2014 Changes from 2012 (+/-)
General Support Services	($000)	12,631	12,607	+2,690	-1,386	13,911	+1,304
	FTE		0	0	-	0	-

SUMMARY OF FY 2014 PROGRAM CHANGES

Request Component	Amount ($000)	FTE
Management Efficiencies	-1,386	
Total:	**-1,386**	**0**

JUSTIFICATION OF FY 2014 PROGRAM CHANGES

The FY 2014 budget request for the General Support Services Activity is $13,911,000 and 0 FTE, a net program decrease of $1,386,000 compared with the FY 2012 Enacted.

Management Efficiencies (-$1,386,000): Programs will absorb these costs through greater efficiencies, cost savings, and administrative adjustments.

PROGRAM OVERVIEW

The General Support Services Activity provides Bureau-wide infrastructure support to both BSEE and BOEM. This activity funds actual infrastructure costs associated with office space, security, utilities, and voice/data communications for all organizational needs to carry out the Bureaus' primary missions.

Funding for shared activities and related support services for both BSEE and BOEM is used for:

- Rental and security of office space
- Workers' compensation and unemployment compensation
- Voice and Data Communications
- The Department's Working Capital Fund (WCF)
- Annual building maintenance contracts
- Mail services
- Printing costs

The two major program objectives are to provide safe and secure facilities that will contribute to the productivity and efficiency of the employees in achieving goals and objectives, and to provide appropriate services in support of the BSEE and BOEM operating programs.

Executive Direction

FY 2014 PERFORMANCE BUDGET REQUEST

Executive Direction Activity

Table 12: Executive Direction Budget Summary

		2013 Full Year CR	2012 Enacted	Fixed Costs (+/-)	Program Changes (+/-)	2014 Budget Request	2014 Changes from 2012 (+/-)
Executive Direction	($000)	18,202	18,117	+118	-114	18,121	+4
	FTE [1]	94	82	0	+10	92	+10

[1] 2012 FTE amounts reflect actual usage, not 2012 enacted formulation estimates.

SUMMARY OF FY 2014 PROGRAM CHANGES

Request Component	Amount ($000)	FTE
Management Efficiencies	-114	
FTE technical adjustment		+10
Total:	**-114**	**+10**

JUSTIFICATION OF FY 2014 PROGRAM CHANGES

The FY 2014 budget request for the Executive Direction Activity is $18,121,000 and 92 FTE, a net program change of -$114,000 and +10 FTE over the FY 2012 Enacted.

Management Efficiencies (-$114,000): Programs will absorb these costs through greater efficiencies, cost savings, and administrative adjustments.

FTE technical adjustment (+10 FTE)

The technical adjustment of 10 FTE represents the difference between 2012 actual and enacted FTE as a result of challenges filling vacant technical positions. No additional funding is requested/associated with this adjustment.

PROGRAM OVERVIEW

The Executive Direction Activity provides Bureau-wide leadership, direction, management, coordination, communications strategies, and outreach for the entire organization to carry out its primary mission. The Executive Direction Activity funds the Office of the Director, the Office of Budget, the Office of Public Affairs, the Office of Policy and Analysis, and the Office of Congressional Affairs.

Office of the Director

The Office of the Director includes the Director, the Deputy Directors, and their immediate staff. This office is responsible for providing general policy guidance and overall leadership within the BSEE organization, as well as managing all of the official documents of the Office of the Director.

Office of Budget

The Office of Budget provides budget analysis and guidance for the formulation, congressional and execution phases of the budget cycle. During the budget formulation cycle, the office develops and maintains all budgetary data to support BSEE's budget requests to the Department with submission of the Budget Proposal, to the Office of Management and Budget with submission of the Budget Estimates, and to the Congress with submission of the Budget Justifications. During the congressional phase, the Office of Budget prepares capability and effect statements, provides answers to House and Senate questions and drafts testimony and oral statements for congressional hearings. Throughout the execution phase, the Budget Division tracks spending against line item budgets, analyzes budgetary and expense data, and provides regular updates to BSEE executives on the status of funds. The Office of Budget works closely with the Office of Policy and Analysis and program level performance staff to integrate performance data and information into all aspects of budget formulation and execution.

Office of Public Affairs (OPA)

The OPA is responsible for BSEE's communication strategies and outreach. The goal of OPA is to inform the public, ensure coordinated communication, consistent messages, and the effective exchange of information with all customers and stakeholders. The OPA coordinates the implementation of an effective and inclusive outreach program to numerous target audiences, including state and local governments, the energy industry, related trade associations, the environmental community, Indian tribes, energy consumer groups and the public.

Office of Policy and Analysis

The Office of Policy and Analysis serves as the principle office to provide the Director with independent review and analysis of programmatic and management issues. Additionally, the office leads, coordinates, and monitors many cross-program initiatives, assuring a consistent, BSEE-wide implementation that directly supports congressional, Presidential and departmental directives, laws, mandates and guidance.

The Office of Policy and Analysis fulfills the Director's responsibilities in several critical areas including strategic and performance planning, policy and program evaluation and internal controls. It is also responsible for ensuring that programmatic plans and policies are consistent with and integrated into the overall Bureau mission and responsibilities, as well as with Department and Administration policy frameworks. In addition, the office administers and coordinates internal reviews, and oversees and assures implementation of recommendations made by oversight groups such as the Government Accountability Office and the Office of Inspector General (OIG).

Office of Congressional Affairs (OCA)

The OCA serves as the primary point of contact with Congress, and is responsible for the coordination of all communication and outreach with congressional offices, as well as ensuring a consistent message and the effective exchange of information. The OCA serves as the liaison for BSEE on all congressional and legislative matters that affect BSEE with Congress, the Department, and other Federal executive agencies.

Investigations and Review Unit (IRU)

The IRU serves as a team of professionals with law enforcement backgrounds or technical expertise whose mission is to: promptly and credibly respond to allegations or evidence of misconduct and unethical behavior by Bureau employees; pursue allegations of misconduct by oil and gas companies involved in offshore energy projects; and assure the Bureau's ability to respond swiftly to emerging issues and crises, including significant incidents such as spills and accidents. The IRU evaluates all information submitted and where appropriate conducts further investigation. The IRU shares allegations of misconduct with the DOI's OIG, and determining jointly which office conducts any investigation of those allegations.

Office of International Programs

The Office of International Programs serves as the primary point of contact between BSEE and the U.S. Department of State (DOS) and its Embassies and the international programs within the Department and other Federal agencies such as the Department of Energy, Department of Commerce, Department of Treasury, etc. The office becomes involved in international initiatives, trends, and developments which promote best practices and better integration of safety, environmental protection, and resource management in offshore energy activities. The office facilitates technical and information exchanges with key national offshore safety authorities across the world and coordinates technical advice to developing countries at the request of DOS. Once the "Agreement between the United States of America and the United Mexican States Concerning Transboundary Hydrocarbon Reservoirs in the Gulf of Mexico" is executed, BSEE's responsibilities will include the approval of unitization agreements, allocation of production, metering of production, inspection of facilities, and safety and environmental enforcement.

Under this Agreement, BSEE will also have responsibilities for the data sharing provisions. Responsibilities also include reporting all BSEE international engagements; advising BSEE and international travelers on matters of security, protocol, and travel requirements; structuring international Memoranda of Understanding and other international cooperation agreements; and coordinating BSEE programs for visiting international delegations. The office maintains an open line of communication regarding BSEE programs and policies to DOS and all relevant U.S. agencies and maintains close liaison with the Department's Office of International Affairs. The Office of International Programs also provides the same functions to the Bureau of Ocean Energy Management.

This page intentionally left blank.

Oil Spill Research

FY 2014 PERFORMANCE BUDGET REQUEST
Oil Spill Research Appropriation

Table 13: Oil Spill Research Budget Summary

		2013 Full Year CR	2012 Enacted	Fixed Costs (+/-)	Program Changes (+/-)	2014 Budget Request	2014 Changes from 2012 (+/-)
Oil Spill Research	($000)	*14,990*	14,899	-	-	14,899	-
	FTE [1/]	*22*	17	-	+5	22	+5

[1/] 2012 FTE amounts reflect actual usage, not 2012 enacted formulation estimates.

SUMMARY OF FY 2014 PROGRAM CHANGES

Request Component	Amount ($000)	FTE
FTE technical adjustment	-	+5
Total:	**+0**	**+5**

JUSTIFICATION OF FY 2014 PROGRAM CHANGES

The FY 2014 budget request for the Oil Spill Appropriation is $14,899,000 and 22 FTE, a net increase of 5 FTE over the FY 2012 Enacted.

FTE technical adjustment (+5 FTE)

The technical adjustment of 5 FTE represents the difference between 2012 actual and enacted FTE as a result of challenges filling vacant technical positions. No additional funding is requested/associated with this adjustment.

PROGRAM OVERVIEW

The Oil Spill Research (OSR) appropriation funds oil spill response research, Ohmsett – the National Oil Spill Response & Renewable Energy Test Facility, and oil spill prevention, planning, preparedness, and response functions for all facilities seaward of the coastline of the United States that handle, store, or transport oil. These activities support the DOI strategic mission of protection of environmental resources and economic interests of the Nation.

Funding for OSR activities is appropriated from the Oil Spill Liability Trust Fund (OSLTF). As intended by the Oil Pollution Act of 1990, the companies that produce and transport oil are supporting research to improve oil spill response capabilities.

PERFORMANCE OVERVIEW

In October 2011, BSEE formally came into existence and established the Oil Spill Response Division (OSRD). This division maintains two focuses; oil spill response research (OSRR) and oil spill response compliance. These two areas support the Strategic Plan BSEE is currently establishing and are influenced by this plan's direction.

The research mission involves coordination with other federal partners. This is achieved through representation in the Interagency Coordinating Committee on Oil Pollution Research (ICCOPR) to identify national priorities for oil spill response research and working with Canadian partners who are developing a Five-Year Strategic Plan for Oil Spill Research in Canadian Arctic Waters. Internally, BSEE, through the Response Research Unit is conducting the foundational work to move research and development projects into innovative new methods to respond to an oil spill.

The OSR funding is used to improve the ability to effectively remove oil from water and protect the environment when oil is discharged from offshore oil facilities. This need is highlighted in the many lessons learned from the Deepwater Horizon incident. Weaknesses and gaps specifically in mechanical and alternative response technologies are noted in the Incident Specific Preparedness Review, the Deepwater Horizon Federal On-Scene Coordinator report, and a report by the National Incident Commander during this spill of national significance. Research will be focused on improving those response tactics such as offshore in situ burn and subsea dispersant use that were found to be viable options. Funding will also be dedicated to finding new and more efficient ways to locate oil and communicate a common operations picture during spill responses. Responding to an oil spill in the Arctic environment presents many unique challenges and funding will be utilized to understand these implications and advance response technologies and procedures to ensure the least impact to the environment and to human safety.

In addition to the oil spill research described below, BSEE Safety and Engineering Research in the Emerging Technologies (formerly the Technology Assessment and Research) program includes technical studies to understand the technology that industry employees use to prevent an oil spill from happening such as blow-out preventers (BOPs) and well- bore cementing procedures.

Oil Spill Response and Planning: BSEE is responsible for ensuring offshore operators have the capability to respond to some of the largest potential oil spills in the Nation. The OSRD compliance staff (10 FTE nationally), provides continuous federal oversight that requires reoccurring compliance actions during the entire lifecycle of offshore oil and gas facilities, from drilling a well to decommissioning and removal. OSRD conducts over 160 plan reviews a year which are required to maintain oversight responsibilities for the nearly 200 approved Oil Spill Response Plans (OSRPs) as operators maintain their content. OSRD staff also conducts equipment validation inspections at over 60 locations, attend 35 industry led exercises, and initiate 25 unannounced government led exercises each year to validate readiness nationwide.

Internal and external coordination is imperative to strengthening the Nation's readiness for an oil spill. BSEE staff participates in Area Committees, Regional Response Teams, and in the National Response Team to represent issues pertaining to offshore. BSEE collaborates with other federal and State response agencies when reviewing oil spill response plans. BSEE also collaborates with international partners. Internally, OSRD is working with other BSEE divisions to proactively identify spills that were not reported in order to take enforcement actions for notification violations. During responses to incidents offshore, BSEE supports all levels of response organizations as subject matter experts in offshore oil spill response.

Oil Spill Response Research (OSRR): BSEE is the principal federal agency funding offshore oil spill response research and has maintained a comprehensive, long-term research program to improve oil spill response technologies and procedures since the 1970's. The OSRR program provides research leadership and funding to improve the knowledge and capability for the detection, containment, and cleanup of oil spills that may occur on the OCS. The program seeks to develop communication technologies such as the use of satellite imagery, side looking infrared radar, and other remote sensing tools. Specific research efforts focused on geographic challenges include Arctic environments due to the anticipated increase in offshore drilling.

The OSRR program is responsive to the information and technological needs of the Bureau's regional and district offices and to specific requirements and limitations in the BSEE authority. Information derived from the OSRR program is directly integrated into BSEE's operations and is used in making regulatory decisions pertaining to permit and plan approvals, safety and pollution prevention inspections, enforcement actions, and training requirements. Research results are also transferred to rule writers, investigators, plan reviewers, and others that need this information to ensure safe operations and will assist BSEE in its efforts to independently keep pace with industry's technological advancements. Response technologies identified by the OSRR program focus on preventing offshore operational spills from reaching sensitive environments and habitats.

The OSRR program is cooperative in nature, bringing together funding and expertise from research partners in government agencies, the oil industry, and the international community through cooperative research arrangements and participation in concurrent research and development projects. Many OSRR projects are Joint Industry Projects (JIP), where BSEE partners with other stakeholders to maximize research dollars.

The current OSRR projects cover a wide spectrum of oil spill response issues and include laboratory, meso-scale and full-scale field experiments. Recent oil spill response research examples include methods to:
- determine the dispersant effectiveness when applied via subsea injection methods, its impact on worker safety by reducing the Volatile Organic Compounds (VOC) that rise to the surface of the water, and modeling efforts to forecast how the dispersed oil will travel through the water column
- enhance in situ burning including how to estimate the burn potential in icy waters
- detect and quantify oil in the water column in addition to detecting, quantifying, and mapping oil in and under ice
- enhance communication of a common operating picture to all responders
- reduce the impact of hydrate formations on capping stack operations.

In FY 2014, BSEE will continue research to:
- develop, test, and evaluate enhanced mechanical recovery technologies, especially those designed for use in Arctic conditions
- refine capabilities to detect and recover oil in and under ice
- work with our federal and industry partners to establish a viable research plan for an intentional release of oil/gas in the marine environment
- develop command and control systems that incorporate and automate science into the decision-making process during a response.

BSEE disseminates research results and development projects as widely as possible in publications through appropriate scientific and technical journals, technical reports, public information documents, and publication on the BSEE website. The intent is to make this information widely available to oil spill response personnel and organizations world-wide.

Ohmsett - The National Oil Spill Response and Renewable Energy Test Facility: Ohmsett is one of the world's largest tow/wave tanks, designed to test and evaluate full scale equipment detection for the cleanup of oil spill containment. Ohmsett is the only facility where oil spill response testing, training, and research can be conducted with a variety of crude oils and refined products in varying wave conditions. The heart of Ohmsett is a large outdoor, above ground concrete test tank that is 667 feet long, 65 feet wide, 11 feet deep and filled with 2.6 million gallons of crystal clear saltwater. Ohmsett also has the capability to test scaled renewable energy systems such as wave generating systems. No other agency operates a facility like Ohmsett.

Ohmsett plays an important role in developing the most effective response technologies, as well as preparing responders with the most realistic training available. The facility provides testing and research capabilities to help the government fulfill its regulatory requirements and meet its goal of clean and safe operations. Major federal clients such as the United States Coast Guard (USCG) and the United States Navy (USN) rely on Ohmsett for their training needs.

Many of today's commercially available oil spill cleanup products have been tested at Ohmsett and a considerable body of performance data and information on mechanical response equipment has been obtained there. This information is used by response planners in reviewing and approving facility response and contingency plans. Ohmsett is also the premier training site for government agency and private industry oil spill response personnel to test their own full-scale equipment. Some of the more recent testing activities included oil spill response equipment testing in a simulated arctic environment, remote sensing tests, wave energy conversion device tests, skimmer and boom tests, dispersant tests, alternative fuel recovery tests, and industry oil spill response training classes.

Due to the facility's coastal location, the effects of Hurricane Sandy were unavoidable. Damage sustained from wind, storm surge, and debris caused the facility to temporarily leave operational status. The facility was returned to operational status within 3 weeks. While the number of days Ohmsett will be available in FY 2013 was reduced by the storm, the tank utilization rate of its operational days is not expected to be impacted. BSEE is coordinating its construction efforts with the National Park Service in order to return the facility to pre Hurricane Sandy condition.

The Ohmsett facility requires constant maintenance, and periodic upgrades. The FY 2013 feasibility studies will determine the necessary upgrades to add the capability for conducting research associated with subsea dispersant injection, and containment of the particulate matter generated by burning oils. Information on Ohmsett can be found at www.ohmsett.com.

Figure 2: Ohmsett Facility in New Jersey

Table 14: Performance Overview Table- Oil Spill Research Appropriation

Supporting Performance Measures	Type	2008 Actual	2009 Actual	2010 Actual	2011 Actual	2012 Plan	2012 Actual	FY 2013 Plan	FY 2014 President's Budget	Change from 2013 to 2014 Plan	Long-term Target 2016
Achieve a utilization rate of X% at Ohmsett, the national oil spill response test facility (BUR)	A	90% (217/240)	86.2% (207/240)	93% (222/240)	84% (202/240)	85%	94% (226/240)	85%	85%	0%	TBD
Contributing Programs	Oil Spill Research										
Comments	*Ohmsett is the National Oil Spill Response Test Facility located in New Jersey. At Ohmsett, clients can test oil spill response equipment in realistic conditions and have training in the use of the equipment. This measure evaluates the utilization level of the facility. The increased focus on oil spill response, as well as expanded uses for the facility such as dispersant training and renewable energy wave tests, have sustained overall utilization rates at around 85%. While the number days Ohmsett will be available in FY 2013 was reduced by Hurricane Sandy, the tank utilization rate of its operational days is not expected to be impacted.*										

This page intentionally left blank.

Appendices

Bureau of Safety and Environmental Enforcement
Section 405 Compliance

Deductions, Reserves, or Holdbacks	FY 2014 ($ Millions)
General Support Services	
Working Capital Fund Centralized Billing	3.5
Working Capital Fund Direct Billing	1.2

Total Assessments of Bureau Programs: $4.7 million

Working Capital Fund - The estimated cost from the Department in providing BSEE with centralized business and administrative services. These charges are paid from the General Support Services activity for the entire Bureau.

BSEE direct bills its activities for support costs and is reimbursed by BOEM for providing administrative services.

Bureau of Safety and Environmental Enforcement
Working Capital Fund Centralized Bill
(Dollars in thousands)

Account	2012 Actual	2013 Estimate	2014 Estimate
Document Management Unit	2.1	42.5	0.0
FOIA Tracking & Reporting System	14.9	16.1	52.9
Alaska Affairs Office	7.4	7.5	8.9
Alaska Resources Library and Information Services	43.2	41.0	43.6
Departmental News and Information	8.4	9.0	7.8
Departmental Museum	12.7	15.2	13.0
FedCenter	2.2	2.1	2.2
Compliance Support ESF-11/ESF-11 Website	0.0	2.3	2.3
Invasive Species Council	17.9	17.2	18.0
Invasive Species Coordinator	3.2	3.2	3.3
Passport and Visa Services	0.0	8.6	8.3
CPIC	1.7	2.2	2.5
Financial Internal Controls & Performance Reporting	10.5	9.6	8.8
Travel Management Center	0.8	0.9	0.8
e-Travel (Formerly: e-Gov Travel)	3.5	14.8	8.4
Interior Collections Management System	2.2	2.1	2.1
Space Management Initiative	3.3	3.6	3.7
FBMS Master Data Systems & Hosting	0.5	14.1	10.9
Planning and Performance Management	11.3	13.6	12.2
Department-wide OWCP Coordination	3.0	2.9	2.7
OPM Federal Employment Services	4.2	4.2	4.2
Accessible Technology Center	3.3	3.5	3.6
Accountability Team	4.9	6.9	5.4
Employee and Labor Relations Tracking System	0.3	0.3	0.3
Veterans Disabilities Hiring Programs	0.0	0.0	2.5
EEO Complaints Tracking System	0.6	0.6	0.6
Special Emphasis Program	0.5	0.5	0.5
Occupational Safety and Health	16.8	19.0	17.2
Safety Management Information System	13.3	14.6	12.5
DOI Learn	15.3	0.0	0.0
Leadership Development (Formerly: DOI Executive Forums)	1.3	8.7	8.2
SESCDP & Other Leadership Programs	1.8	0.0	0.0
Dept-Wide Training Programs (including Online Learning)	5.0	24.7	21.8
Learning and Performance Center Management	4.1	0.0	0.0
Albuquerque Learning & Performance Center	2.8	2.7	2.7
Anchorage Learning & Performance Center	5.1	0.0	0.0

Bureau of Safety and Environmental Enforcement
Working Capital Fund Centralized Bill
(Dollars in thousands)

Account	2012 Actual	2013 Estimate	2014 Estimate
Washington Learning & Performance Center	12.1	11.9	11.9
DOIU Management	5.8	8.2	8.3
Security (Classified Information Facility)	5.5	5.5	6.0
Law Enforcement Coordination and Training	10.6	10.1	9.0
Security (MIB/SIB Complex)	144.7	144.7	157.6
Victim Witness	2.0	2.0	1.9
Interior Operations Center	30.3	24.6	21.9
Emergency Preparedness	9.8	9.3	10.3
Emergency Response	13.6	12.9	15.6
MIB Health and Safety	2.4	2.9	3.3
Federal Executive Board	0.0	3.4	3.1
Aviation Management	0.0	386.0	858.7
Electronic Records Management	8.2	12.7	19.6
TELECOM - Enterprise Services Network	186.1	174.8	180.6
INFO ASSURANCE - Web & Internal/External Comm	5.5	5.0	4.4
Enterprise Architecture	37.1	31.6	34.5
IT Security-IVV	24.2	19.1	21.0
Capital Planning	17.9	23.1	25.7
INFO ASSURANCE - Privacy (Information Management Support)	7.2	4.1	8.2
IT Security – Information Assurance Division	50.9	10.5	12.1
END USER SVCS - Active Directory	33.5	34.0	25.2
Enterprise Resource Management	4.7	11.1	17.5
INFO ASSURANCE - DOI Access & Personnel Security	12.8	11.5	12.6
Data at Rest	0.6	0.0	0.0
END USER SVCS - IT Asset Management	3.4	8.6	9.3
OCIO Project Management Office	8.2	0.0	0.0
INFO ASSURANCE - Threat Management	9.0	25.1	25.5
END USER SVCS - IOS Collaboration	9.3	8.4	9.6
END USER SVCS - Unified Messaging	19.4	17.4	7.9
TELECOM - Federal Relay Service	0.4	0.3	0.3
IT Transformation (ITT)	0.0	0.0	185.5
HOSTING - Cloud Services	0.0	0.0	14.6
ITD IT Security Improvement Plan	0.0	0.0	7.6
ITD MIB Data Networking	0.0	0.0	10.7
ITD Information Management - Records Management	0.0	0.0	15.3
ITD Telecommunication Services	0.0	0.0	24.6
ITD Integrated Digital Voice Communications System	0.0	0.0	17.4
ITD Desktop Services	0.0	0.0	3.4

Bureau of Safety and Environmental Enforcement
Working Capital Fund Centralized Bill
(Dollars in thousands)

Account	2012 Actual	2013 Estimate	2014 Estimate
FBMS Help Desk – Customer Support Center	0.0	0.0	126.1
Alternative Dispute Resolution (ADR) Training	0.6	0.6	0.5
Mail and Messenger Services	0.0	32.0	42.7
Health Unit	0.0	6.2	6.4
Special Event Services	0.0	1.0	0.9
Safety and Environmental Services	0.0	10.2	10.5
Shipping and Receiving	0.0	7.1	7.3
Vehicle Fleet	0.0	1.9	1.8
Property Accountability Services	0.0	13.5	14.0
Family Support Room	0.0	0.6	0.6
Interior Complex Management & Services	0.0	18.8	19.5
Departmental Library	0.0	28.6	10.0
Mail Policy	0.0	4.2	3.7
Moving Services	0.0	5.1	5.3
Passport and Visa Services	0.0	0.0	0.0
Audio Visual Services	0.0	26.3	28.7
Federal Executive Board	0.0	0.0	0.0
Space Management Services	0.0	6.8	7.0
Conservation and Education Partnerships	3.2	2.9	2.7
Contingency Reserve	1.9	1.8	1.6
Cooperative Ecosystem Study Units	10.0	10.0	21.2
CFO Financial Statement Audit	538.6	542.2	535.9
e-Government Initiatives (WCF Contributions Only)	32.9	48.8	51.1
Ethics	7.4	6.6	5.6
FOIA Appeals	11.6	10.4	22.0
IBC IT Security Improvement Plan	7.5	7.5	0.0
MIB Data Networking	9.9	9.8	0.0
Information Management - Records Management	6.2	6.2	0.0
Telecommunication Services	37.2	22.4	0.0
Integrated Digital Voice Communications System	18.6	17.3	0.0
Desktop Services	4.6	3.4	0.0
Interior Complex Cabling O&M	1.3	0.0	0.0
Audio Visual Services	7.1	0.0	0.0
FPPS/Employee Express - O&M	139.9	136.8	136.8
Departmental Library	29.3	0.0	0.0
Interior Complex Management & Services	18.3	0.0	0.0
Family Support Room	0.7	0.0	0.0
Property Accountability Services	13.7	0.0	0.0
Vehicle Fleet	2.0	0.0	0.0

Bureau of Safety and Environmental Enforcement
Working Capital Fund Centralized Bill
(Dollars in thousands)

Account	2012 Actual	2013 Estimate	2014 Estimate
Moving Services	5.2	0.0	0.0
Shipping and Receiving	7.2	0.0	0.0
Safety and Environmental Services	10.3	0.0	0.0
Space Management	6.9	0.0	0.0
Federal Executive Board	3.4	0.0	0.0
Health Unit	6.3	0.0	0.0
Mail & Messenger Services	28.2	0.0	0.0
Mail Policy	4.3	0.0	0.0
Special Events Services	1.1	0.0	0.0
Passport and Visa Services	8.7	0.0	0.0
Transportation Services (Household Goods)	1.6	1.7	1.7
IDEAS	8.4	7.0	2.9
FBMS Master Data Management	0.4	0.4	0.5
IBC FBMS Conversion	3.4	0.0	0.0
Consolidated Financial Statement System	8.4	8.4	6.7
Aviation Management	431.9	0.0	0.0
Aviation Management System - O&M	23.2	0.0	0.0
Boise Acquisition Office	0.0	70.0	196.3
FBMS Hosting / Applications Management	184.5	64.5	68.3
FBMS Redirect - IDEAS	27.6	29.1	33.2
FBMS Help Desk – IBC Customer Support Center	0.0	120.2	0.0
TOTAL	**2,576.4**	**2,623.9**	**3,463.9**

Bureau of Safety and Environmental Enforcement
Working Capital Fund Direct Bill
(Dollars in thousands)

Account	2012 Actual	2013 Estimate	2014 Estimate
Ocean Coastal Great Lakes Activities	20.8	0.0	0.0
Federal Assistance Award Data System	0.5	0.0	0.0
e-OPF	0.0	18.2	39.9
EAP Consolidation	0.0	7.1	8.7
Worker's Comp Nurse Case Management	0.0	0.0	2.0
Equal Employment Opportunity (EEO) Training	12.3	12.3	12.3
Albuquerque Learning & Performance Center	2.2	2.4	2.4
Online Learning	6.0	6.0	6.0
Washington Leadership & Performance Center	6.3	6.3	6.3
Anchorage Learning & Performance Center	0.2	0.0	0.0
INFO ASSURANCE – Anti-virus Software Licenses	53.4	19.0	16.4
END USER SVCS – Unified Messaging	264.2	171.6	178.4
INFO ASSURANCE – DOI Access	0.0	44.8	90.0
Data at Rest Initiative	6.0	2.4	2.4
HOSTING – Hosting/Cloud Services	0.0	0.0	17.1
ITD Customer Support Services Division	0.0	0.0	1.1
TELECOM – Enterprise Services Network	311.4	126.8	126.8
Microsoft Enterprise Licenses	306.1	0.0	0.0
Creative Communications Services (CCS)	0.0	5.0	4.9
e-Mail Archiving (Cobell Litigation)	66.5	0.0	0.0
Federal Flexible Savings Account (FSA) Program	9.9	10.1	10.1
ESRI Enterprise Licenses	117.1	47.6	47.6
FBMS Change Orders	11.5	10.2	10.0
Enterprise Technology Division	72.2	0.0	0.0
Customer Support Services Division	2.0	1.1	0.0
Payroll & HR System	108.7	227.8	238.4
Facilities Reimbursable Services	27.6	0.0	0.0
Creative Communications	3.2	0.0	0.0
Reimbursable Mail Services	1.5	0.0	0.0
TOTAL	**1,409.6**	**718.6**	**820.7**

Bureau of Safety and Environmental Enforcement
Employee Count by Grade

Employee Count by Grade
(Total Employment)

	2012 Actuals	2013 Estimates	2014 Estimates
Executive Level V	1	1	1
SES	5	5	5
Subtotal	**6**	**6**	**6**
SL - 00	0	0	0
ST - 00	0	0	0
Subtotal	**0**	**0**	**0**
GS/GM -15	44	44	44
GS/GM -14	120	120	120
GS/GM -13	178	178	178
GS -12	83	83	100
GS -11	80	116	152
GS -10	4	4	4
GS - 9	50	50	50
GS - 8	21	21	21
GS -7	34	34	34
GS - 6	19	19	19
GS - 5	20	20	20
GS - 4	13	13	13
GS - 3	2	2	2
GS - 2	0	0	0
GS -1	0	0	0
Subtotal	**668**	**704**	**757**
Other Pay Schedule Systems	0	0	0
Total employment (actuals & estimates)	**674**	**710**	**763**

This page intentionally left blank.

Bureau of Safety and Environmental Enforcement
Offshore Safety and Environmental Enforcement (OSEE)
MAX Tables and Budget Schedules

Program and Financing *(dollars in millions)*		FY 2012 Actual	FY 2013 Estimate	FY 2014 Estimate
Treasury Account ID: 14-1700				
Obligations by program activity -Direct program				
0001	Appropriations	60	62	83
0002	Offsetting Collections		121	124
0789	**Total direct obligations**	**60**	**183**	**207**
Obligations by program activity -Reimbursable program				
0801	Offsetting collections & Reimbursable Receipts	133		
0802	Reimbursable Service Agreements		33	33
0899	**Total reimbursable obligations**	**133**	**33**	**33**
0900	**Total new obligations (direct & reimbursable)**	**193**	**216**	**240**
Budgetary resources				
1000	Unobligated balance brought forward, Oct 1		69	69
1011	Unobligated balance transfer from account [14-1917] *	36		
1050	**Unobligated balance (total)**	**36**	**69**	**69**
Budget authority				
1160	**Appropriation, discretionary**	**61**	**62**	**83**
Spending authority from offsetting collections, discretionary				
1700	Spending authority from offsetting collections (Cost Recovery)		6	8
1700	Spending authority from offsetting collections (Rents-Cost Recovery)	59	53	51
1700	Collected (Inspection Fees)	23		65
1701	Change in uncollected payments, Federal sources	21		
1700	Spending authority from offsetting collections (Reimbursable Service Agreements)		33	33
1711	Spending authority from offsetting collections transferred from account [14-1917]	62	62	
1750	**Total spending authority from offsetting collections, discretionary**	**165**	**154**	**157**
1900	**Budget authority (total)**	**226**	**216**	**240**
1050	Unobligated balance	36	69	69
1930	**Total budgetary resources**	**262**	**285**	**309**
0900	Obligations incurred, unexpired accounts	-193	-216	-240
1941	**Unobligated balance carried forward, end of year**	**69**	**69**	**69**
Net budget authority and outlays				
4180	Budget authority, net (total)	123	124	83
4190	Outlays, net (total)	43	129	79
* Unobligated Balance of $36M was brought forward from BOEMRE and transferred from BOEM to BSEE. FY 2012 is the first year of BSEE.				

Bureau of Safety and Environmental Enforcement
Offshore Safety and Environmental Enforcement (OSEE)

Object Classification *(dollars in millions)*			
Treasury Account ID: 14-1700	**FY 2012 Actual**	**FY 2013 Estimate**	**FY 2014 Estimate**
OSEE (Direct Obligations)			
11 Personnel Compensation: Full-time permanent	32	46	52
12 Civilian personnel benefits	11	16	17
21 Travel and transportation of persons	1	4	4
23 Rental payments to GSA	1	8	8
25 Other services	9	105	122
26 Supplies and materials	1	1	1
31 Equipment	5	3	3
OSEE (Reimbursable Obligations)			
11 Personnel Compensation: Full-time permanent	16	10	10
12 Civilian personnel benefits	5	4	4
21 Travel and transportation of persons	1		
23 Rental payments to GSA	14	6	6
25 Other services	91	13	13
26 Supplies and materials	1		
31 Equipment	5		
99.0 Total OSEE	**193**	**216**	**240**

Bureau of Safety and Environmental Enforcement
Oil Spill Research (OSR)

Program and Financing
(dollars in millions)

Treasury Account ID: 14-8370		FY 2012 Actual	FY 2013 Estimate	FY 2014 Estimate
Obligations by program activity -Direct program				
0001	Direct program activity	12	15	15
0900	**Total new obligations**	**12**	**15**	**15**
Budgetary resources				
1000	Unobligated balance brought forward, Oct 1	3	6	6
1101	Appropriation (special or trust fund)	15	15	15
1930	**Total budgetary resources**	**18**	**21**	**21**
0900	Obligations incurred, unexpired accounts	12	15	15
1941	**Unobligated balance carried forward, end of year**	**6**	**6**	**6**
Net budget authority and outlays				
4180	Budget authority, net (total)	15	15	15
4190	Outlays, net (total)	10	14	15

Object Classification
(dollars in millions)

Treasury Account ID: 14-8370		FY 2012 Actual	FY 2013 Estimate	FY 2014 Estimate
OSR (Direct Obligations)				
11	Personnel Compensation: Full-time permanent	2	2	2
12	Civilian Personnel Benefits		1	1
25	Other services	8	12	12
94	Financial Transfers*	1		
OSR (Reimbursable Obligations)				
25	Other services	*1*		
99.0	**Total OSR**	*12*	*15*	*15*
	Transfer of $1M to BOEM.			

Bureau of Safety and Environmental Enforcement
Oil Spill Research (OSR)
Disaster Relief Appropriations Act, 2013 (P.L. 113-2)

Program and Financing
(dollars in millions)

Treasury Account ID: 14-1920	FY 2012 Actual	FY 2013 Estimate	FY 2014 Estimate
Obligations by program activity -Direct program			
0001 Direct program activity		3	
0900 Total new obligations		**3**	
Budgetary resources			
1100 Appropriation		3	
1930 Total budgetary resources		**3**	
Net budget authority and outlays			
4180 Budget authority, net (total)		3	
4190 Outlays, net (total)		1	2

Object Classification
(dollars in millions)

Treasury Account ID: 14-1920	FY 2012 Actual	FY 2013 Estimate	FY 2014 Estimate
OSR (Direct Obligations)			
25 Other services		3	

Bureau of Safety and Environmental Enforcement
Authorizing Statutes

Outer Continental Shelf (OCS) Lands Program

43 U.S.C. 1331, et seq.	The Outer Continental Shelf (OCS) Lands Act of 1953, as amended, extended the jurisdiction of the United States to the OCS and provided for granting of leases to develop offshore energy and minerals.
P.L. 109-432	The Gulf of Mexico Energy Security Act of 2006 required leasing certain areas in the Central and Eastern Gulf of Mexico Planning Areas within one year of enactment (December 20, 2006); and established a moratoria on leasing in remaining areas in the eastern planning area and a portion of the central planning area until 2022.
P.L. 109-58	The Energy Policy Act of 2005 amended the OCS Lands Act to give authority to the Department of the Interior to coordinate the development of an alternative energy program on the OCS and also to coordinate the energy and non-energy related uses in areas of the OCS where traditional oil and natural gas development already occur.
43 U.S.C. 4321, 4331-4335, 4341-4347	The National Environmental Policy Act of 1969 required that federal agencies consider in their decisions the environmental effects of proposed activities and that Agencies prepare environmental impact statements for Federal actions having a significant effect on the environment.
16 U.S.C. 1451, et seq.	The Coastal Zone Management Act of 1972, as amended, established goals for ensuring that Federal and industry activity in the coastal zone be consistent with coastal zone plans set by the States.
16 U.S.C. 1531-1543	The Endangered Species Act of 1973 established procedures to ensure interagency cooperation and consultations to protect endangered and threatened species.
42 U.S.C. 7401, et seq.	The Clean Air Act, as amended, was applied to all areas of the OCS except the central and western Gulf of Mexico. OCS activities in those non-excepted areas will require pollutant emission permits administered by the EPA or the States.
P. L. 112-42, Section 432	Consolidated Appropriations Act of 2012, amended the Clean Air Act by transferring air quality jurisdiction from the EPA to DOI for OCS activities in the Beaufort Sea and Chukchi Sea OCS Planning Areas of the Arctic OCS.

16 U.S.C. 470-470W6	The <u>National Historic Preservation Act</u> established procedures to ensure protection of significant archaeological resources.
30 U.S.C. 21(a)	The <u>Mining and Minerals Policy Act of 1970</u> set forth the continuing policy of the Federal Government to foster and encourage private enterprise in the orderly and economic development of domestic mineral resources and reserves.
30 U.S.C. 1601	The <u>Policy, Research and Development Act of 1970</u> set forth the continuing policy <u>et seq.</u> of the Federal Government to foster and encourage private enterprise in the orderly and economic development of domestic mineral resources and reserves.
33 U.S.C. 2701, <u>et seq.</u>	The <u>Oil Pollution Act of 1990</u> established a fund for compensation of damages resulting from oil pollution and provided for interagency coordination and for the performance of oil spill prevention and response research. It also expanded coverage of Federal requirements for oil spill response planning to include State waters and the transportation of oil. The Act also addressed other related regulatory issues.
43 U.S.C. 1301	The <u>Marine Protection, Research, and Sanctuaries Act of 1972</u> provided that the Secretary of Commerce must consult with the Secretary of the Interior prior to designating marine sanctuaries. BSEE provides oversight and enforcement for potential impacts from all OCS activities that may be located in or in proximity to marine sanctuaries and protected areas.
16 U.S.C. 1361-1362, 1371-1384, 1401-1407	The <u>Marine Mammal Protection Act of 1972</u> provides for the protection and welfare of marine mammals.
P.L. 104-58	The <u>Deepwater Royalty Relief Act</u> provides royalty rate relief for offshore drilling in deepwater of the Gulf of Mexico (GOM).
31 U.S.C. 9701	<u>Fees and Charges for Government Services and Things of Value.</u> It establishes authority for Federal agencies to collect fees for services provided by the Government. Those fees must be fair and based on the costs to the Government; the value of the services or thing to the recipient; public policy or interest served; and other relevant facts.

General Administration

31 U.S.C. 65	<u>Budget and Accounting Procedures Act of 1950</u>
31 U.S.C. 3901-3906	<u>Prompt Payment Act of 1982</u>
31 U.S.C. 3512	<u>Federal Managers Financial Integrity Act of 1982</u>
5 U.S.C. 552	<u>Freedom of Information Act of 1966, as amended</u>

31 U.S.C. 7501-7507	Single Audit Act of 1984
41 U.S.C. 35045	Walsh Healy Public Contracts Act of 1936
41 U.S.C. 351-357	Service Contract Act of 1965
41 U.S.C. 601-613	Contract Disputes Act of 1978
44 U.S.C. 35	Paperwork Reduction Act of 1980
44 U.S.C. 2101	Federal Records Act 1950
40 U.S.C. 4868	Federal Acquisition Regulation of 1984
31 U.S.C. 3501	Privacy Act of 1974
31 U.S.C. 3501	Accounting and Collection
31 U.S.C. 3711, 3716-19	Claims
31 U.S.C. 1501-1557	Appropriation Accounting
5 U.S.C. 1104 et seq.	Delegation of Personnel Management Authority
31 U.S.C. 665-665(a)	Anti-Deficiency Act of 1905, as amended
41 U.S.C. 252	Competition in Contracting Act of 1984
18 U.S.C. 1001	False Claims Act of 1982
18 U.S.C. 287	False Statements Act of 1962
41 U.S.C. 501-509	Federal Grant and Cooperative Agreement Act of 1977
41 U.S.C. 253	Federal Property and Administrative Services Act of 1949
41 U.S.C. 401	Office of Federal Procurement Policy Act of 1974, as amended
15 U.S.C. 631	Small Business Act of 1953, as amended
15 U.S.C. 637	Small Business Act Amendments of 1978
10 U.S.C. 137	Small Business and Federal Competition Enhancement Act of 1984
15 U.S.C. 638	Small Business Innovation Research Program of 1983
10 U.S.C. 2306(f)	Truth in Negotiations Act of 1962 Authorization

Secretarial Order No. 3299	Directed the creation of the Bureau of Ocean Energy Management, the Bureau of Safety and Environmental Enforcement, and the Office of Natural Resources Revenue in May 2010, under the authority provided by Section 2 of Reorganization Plan No. 3 of 1950 (64 Stat. 1262).
Secretarial Order No. 3302	Changed the Name of the Minerals Management Service to the Bureau of Ocean Energy Management, Regulation and Enforcement in June 2010, under the authority provided by Section 2 of Reorganization Plan No. 3 of 1950 (64 Stat. 1262).

Oil Spill Research

33 U.S.C. 2701, et seq.	Title VII of the Oil Pollution Act of 1990 authorizes the use of the Oil Spill Liability Trust fund, established by Section 9505 of the Internal Revenue Code of 1986, for oil spill research.
33 U.S.C. 2701, et seq.	Title I, Section 1016, of the Oil Pollution Act of 1990 requires a certification process which ensures that each responsible company, with respect to an offshore facility, has established, and maintains, evidence of financial responsibility in the amount of at least $150,000,000 to meet potential pollution liability.
43 U.S.C. 1331, et seq.	Section 21(b) of the Outer Continental Shelf Lands Act, as amended, requires the use of the best available and safety technologies (BAST) and assurance that the use of up-to-date technology is incorporated into the regulatory process.
Executive Order 12777	Signed October 18, 1991, assigned the responsibility to ensure oil spill financial responsibility for OCS facilities to the Secretary of the Interior (Bureau of Safety and Environmental Enforcement).